You're Smarter Than You Think

A Kid's Guide to Multiple Intelligences

THOMAS ARMSTRONG, PH.D.

Edited by Jennifer Brannen

free spirit
PUBLISHING®

Helping kids
help themselves™
since 1983

Library of Congress Cataloging-in-Publication Data

Armstrong, Thomas.
    You're smarter than you think : a kid's guide to multiple intelligences / by Thomas Armstrong.
        v. cm.
    Includes bibliographical references and index.
    ISBN 1-57542-113-5
        1. Multiple intelligences—Juvenile literature. [1. Multiple intelligences. 2. Learning strategies.] I. Brannen, Jennifer. II. Title.

BF432.3 .A795 2003
153.9—dc21   2002002687

At the time of this book's publication, all facts and figures cited are the most current available; all telephone numbers, addresses, and Web site URLs are accurate and active; all publications, organizations, Web sites, and other resources exist as described in this book; and all have been verified as of March 2004. The author and Free Spirit Publishing make no warranty or guarantee concerning the information and materials given out by organizations or content found at Web sites, and we are not responsible for any changes that occur after this book's publication. If you find an error or believe that a resource listed here is not as described, please contact Free Spirit Publishing. Parents, teachers, and other adults: We strongly urge you to monitor children's use of the Internet.

Cover and interior book design by Marieka Heinlen
Index compiled by Kay K. Schlembach

10 9 8 7 6 5 4
Printed in Canada

Free Spirit Publishing Inc.
217 Fifth Avenue North, Suite 200
Minneapolis, MN 55401-1299
(612) 338-2068
help4kids@freespirit.com
www.freespirit.com

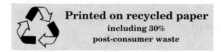

Printed on recycled paper
including 30%
post-consumer waste

green
press
INITIATIVE

Dedication
To Jane

Acknowledgments

I'd like to thank KaTrina Wentzel for using her People Smart to get in touch with me about doing this book for Free Spirit; Jennifer Brannen, for her Word Smart in doing such a great job of editing the text; Marieka Heinlen, for using her Picture Smart to create wonderful images for the book; and Judy Galbraith for her Self Smart vision in creating a publishing company to empower kids in school and in life. Finally, I'd like to thank Dr. Howard Gardner, whose work in multiple intelligences has helped millions of kids worldwide realize how smart they really are!

Contents

Why You're Smarter Than You Think

Do you think you're smart? What does it mean to be smart anyway? Many people believe being smart is all about getting good grades and high test scores in school. Lots of people think being smart means you can do things like:

* read really well

* solve math problems quickly

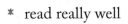

Did you know the names of Popeye's four nephews are Pipeye, Peepeye, Pupeye, and Poopeye!?!

* recite a bunch of facts

* understand everything about computers

So, what do *you* think being smart means?

Here's something that may surprise you: Being smart isn't only about getting good grades, scoring well on tests, and memorizing stuff. In fact, there are lots of other ways to show your smarts—through art, music, athletics, nature, emotions, and getting along with others (to name a few). In this book, you'll discover that there are many ways to be smart.

For about the past 100 years, experts have often used IQ tests to figure out how smart people are. IQ stands for *Intelligence Quotient,* and it is a measure of how someone scores on the test. The test has you solve math problems, define words, create designs, repeat numbers from memory, and do other tasks. Maybe you've taken an IQ test.

Many people think that IQ tests are the best way to measure how smart someone is. IQ tests aren't perfect though, and there's a lot they can't tell you. They can't predict what you'll do when you grow up or what you can achieve in your life. And the test questions may reflect the biases, or opinions, of the people who created them. Besides, no test can test for everything. The questions don't always give you the best chance to show off your different kinds of smarts. IQ tests generally focus most of their attention on being good with words or numbers, and they neglect other important things like music, art, nature, and social ability.

Recently, people have challenged the idea that IQ is the best measure of intelligence. One of those people is a psychologist and a professor of education from Harvard University named Dr. Howard Gardner. Thanks in part to his work, experts now have a whole new idea of what it means to be smart.

The Theory of Multiple Intelligences

Since IQ tests are limited and don't test for the wide range of abilities that people often show and use, Dr. Gardner suggests they aren't a true measure of how smart someone really is.

Dr. Gardner decided there isn't just *one* way to be smart but *many different ways*. He used his research with kids and adults to discover more about how people learn. Dr. Gardner found out that people seemed to learn and show their smarts in a lot of ways. He also noticed that different parts of the brain seemed to be tied to the different ways of being smart. He came up with an idea, or theory, to explain the wide range of abilities he was seeing. He called his idea the *Theory of Multiple Intelligences* (or *MI theory* for short).

If you think about it, Dr. Gardner's idea about different kinds of intelligence makes sense. There are plenty of examples of people who haven't scored well on IQ tests or who haven't even been tested on what they're good at doing, but who are clearly very smart in many other ways. These might include people who paint, climb mountains, make business deals, explore nature, or invent machines. Certainly, you can score well on an IQ test and still do those things, but your test results won't necessarily show everything that you're good at.

MI theory says there are eight different kinds of intelligence—eight ways to be smart! (There may even be more, but they haven't been identified yet.) Each of these different kinds of intelligence can be described by certain traits, activities, and interests.

When Dr. Gardner published books about his theory, he came up with names for the different kinds of intelligences. Here are the eight kinds of smart he talked about: (1) Linguistic Intelligence, (2) Musical

Intelligence, (3) Logical-Mathematical Intelligence, (4) Spatial Intelligence, (5) Bodily-Kinesthetic Intelligence, (6) Interpersonal Intelligence, (7) Intrapersonal Intelligence, and (8) Naturalist Intelligence.

I've been studying Dr. Gardner's work for almost 20 years now. Over the years, I've written many books for adults on multiple intelligences. But because I've also spent many years teaching kids, I wanted to write a book that would help young people. I hope to explain MI theory in a way that makes it easy for you to understand, because I think it's important for kids like you to make the most of *all* your smarts.

To make things easier, I've created some simpler language to describe the eight intelligences:

1 **Word Smart** (Linguistic Intelligence): You like words and how they're used in reading, writing, or speaking. You may enjoy word play and word games, foreign languages, storytelling, spelling, creative writing, or reading. For more about this intelligence, see Chapter 1.

2 **Music Smart** (Musical Intelligence): You appreciate music, rhythm, melody, and patterns in sounds. You are capable of hearing tone and pitch. You may appreciate many different kinds of music and enjoy activities like singing, playing instruments, listening to CDs, or attending concerts. For more about this intelligence, see Chapter 2.

3 **Logic Smart** (Logical-Mathematical Intelligence): You enjoy figuring things out and may understand numbers and math concepts, like finding patterns, and have fun with science. You may like riddles, brainteasers, computers, creating your own codes, or doing science experiments. For more about this intelligence, see Chapter 3.

4 **Picture Smart** (Spatial Intelligence): You love to look at the world and see all the interesting things in it. You may be able to picture things or images in your head. You may be able to take what you see and use your imagination to show others your vision through art, design, photography, architecture, or invention. For more about this intelligence, see Chapter 4.

5 **Body Smart** (Bodily-Kinesthetic Intelligence): You're graceful and comfortable in your body, using it to learn new skills or to express yourself in different ways. You may be an athlete or use your body artistically in dance or acting. Or you may have more interest in working with your hands and doing activities like crafts, building models, or repairing things. For more about this intelligence, see Chapter 5.

6 **People Smart** (Interpersonal Intelligence): You're interested in other people and how people interact with each other. You may be part of student government or a peer mediation group at school, have lots of friends, be involved in neighborhood causes, or just enjoy being in casual social groups. For more about this intelligence, see Chapter 6.

7 **Self Smart** (Intrapersonal Intelligence): You're aware of and understand your own feelings, what you're good at, and the areas you want to improve. You often understand yourself better than others understand you. You may keep a journal, create plans for the future, reflect on the past, or set goals for yourself. For more about this intelligence, see Chapter 7.

8 **Nature Smart** (Naturalist Intelligence): You're observant and enjoy identifying and classifying things like plants, animals, or rocks. (If you live in the city, you may classify other things like CDs or what your classmates wear.) You probably love being outdoors and may be interested in gardening, taking care of pets, cooking, or getting involved in ecological causes. For more about this intelligence, see Chapter 8.

About This Book

The next eight chapters will describe in detail each of the eight ways to be smart. As you read through them, notice where you see yourself most clearly, and where you see your friends, your family, and even your teachers in each of the intelligences. This book will help you learn about who you are and who you can be. Not only that, it will also help you understand and get along better with the people around you—your brothers and sisters, your parents, your friends, your teachers, and others. You'll learn that everyone has different strengths and different ideas about how to do things, which will make it easier to understand them, get along with them, and even learn from them. So maybe this book will help you pick up basketball tips from your Body Smart older sister, learn from your Logic Smart teacher, or get along better with your Self Smart friend.

Here's the good news: *You already have all eight kinds of smart.* Really! You're not just one type of smart. In different degrees, you're smart in *all* of the ways this book describes. This doesn't mean you're great at everything (no one's *that* good); but you *do* have some ability in each area. As you read about the different intelligences, you're probably going to discover that you see at least a little bit of yourself in each of them. So, you're already eight times smarter than you were before you read this.

Here's more good news:

* *All of the intelligences are* **different,** *but they're also* **equal.** No intelligence is better or more important than another.

* *No matter what kind of ability you have in a given smart, you can explore, grow, and develop it.* Whether you have trouble spelling "dictionary" or you're a future best-selling author, you can become more Word Smart. That's just one example, but you get the idea.

* *You may know what you're best at, but that doesn't mean you're limited to one kind of intelligence.* Maybe you're Body Smart— congratulations!—but don't let that keep you from the joys of reading, just because it uses another kind of smart (Word Smart).

* *There are many different ways of being smart in each intelligence.* For example, if you're Word Smart, you might discover that you're a top-notch speaker but not such a terrific writer. Or for Body Smart, you might find you're not very good at soccer but you're a great swimmer. With some work, you can build on your strengths and improve your weaknesses.

* *The different smarts work together in almost everything you do.* For example, you might think that painting a picture is just about being Picture Smart. Wrong! Painting a picture can use Body Smart to master different brush techniques, Nature Smart to develop your eye for detail, or even Self Smart to come up with ideas to paint. Most activities rely on a lot of different smarts, not just the most obvious ones. So just as it takes more than Picture Smart to paint a picture, it usually takes more than one intelligence to do anything—whether it's acting, writing a story, playing hockey, or programming a computer.

* ***The eight intelligences are found across all cultures and in all countries and age groups.*** So no matter who you are or where you're from—no matter what your age or background—you have some form of all of the different intelligences. It's up to you to develop each one as best as you can.

Practically everywhere you look in life you can see signs of multiple intelligences at work. You might see Nature Smart and Picture Smart in your neighbor who has a beautiful garden. You might see Word Smart in your brother who's always writing in his journal, or Music Smart in your mom who loves to sing. You might be learning math at school from a Logic Smart teacher or social studies from a People Smart teacher. You may have a Body Smart friend who juggles, or a Self Smart friend who started her own business. You might see the different intelligences in the Body Smart bus driver who takes you to school, or the People Smart clerk at the grocery store. Everywhere you turn—at home, in your classroom, or in public—you can see the different smarts at work.

Chances are, though, you can see the different smarts most easily in yourself. After all, who do you spend the most time with? Yourself, of course. If the multiple intelligences aren't obvious to you, that's okay. This book will help you recognize and make the most of them.

Each of us uses all eight intelligences every day, but each of us is unique in how we show our smarts. In a way, it's as if the eight intelligences were different notes of an octave on a musical scale: C, D, E, F, G, A, B, C. Each one of us is like a different song made up of those eight notes. The way we combine the notes is unique, so no song is exactly the same. When you use all of your intelligences as much as you can—in your own unique way—you will fill the world with a marvelous tune that nobody else can make!

If you'd like to write to me, I'd love to hear from you. Send letters to:

Dr. Thomas Armstrong
c/o Free Spirit Publishing
217 Fifth Avenue North, Suite 200
Minneapolis, MN 55401-1299

Or email me at: help4kids@freespirit.com.

Chapter 1

Word Smart

Quick Quiz

Do you:

* love to read?
* like to tell stories?
* write stories or poetry?
* enjoy learning foreign languages?
* have a good vocabulary?
* spell well?
* like to write letters or email?
* enjoy talking about ideas with others?
* have a good memory for names or facts?
* play word games such as word scrambles, hidden word puzzles, Scrabble, or crossword puzzles?
* like to do research and read about ideas that interest you?
* have fun playing with words (puns, tongue twisters, and rhymes)?

If you answered yes to any of the questions above, then you just identified some of the ways you're Word Smart!

What Does It Mean to Be Word Smart?

You're Word Smart if you like words and the ways that they can be used in reading, writing, and speaking. You may be sensitive to how words sound, what they mean, and how they are used. You may enjoy playing with words or creating word games. You can show this intelligence by being a good poet or writer, a super speller, a bookworm, an excellent story-teller, a compelling debater, or a whiz at learning languages.

You're already Word Smart whether you realize it or not. By reading this book, even if it's hard for you, you're being Word Smart. When you talk to your family, read the sports page or your favorite comic, or write emails or letters to your friends, you're being Word Smart.

What can being Word Smart do for you?

* You can communicate with others through speaking or writing.

* You can help yourself do well in school. A lot of things you do in school are Word Smart activities—reading, writing, spelling, memorizing facts, making presentations in class, and discussing ideas.

* You can visit new places, meet interesting people, and see mysterious things—all through books.

Things you may do every day that use this intelligence:

read (books, magazines, newspapers, and comics) ▪ write poetry and stories ▪ write and put on skits ▪ keep a journal ▪ tell stories ▪ tell jokes ▪ write letters, notes, and email ▪ speak out for causes you believe in ▪ rap ▪ listen to talk radio or radio shows and plays ▪ watch movies ▪ listen to books on tape

Everybody is Word Smart. If somebody ever comes up to you and says: "I don't think I'm Word Smart" you can say to them, "In order for you to tell me that, you had to be Word Smart!" (Because the person used *words* to communicate.)

THE SPOKEN WORD

Being Word Smart is about good communication skills. What's the simplest way to communicate? By speaking and listening, of course. Those are two things that just about everyone everywhere does every day. Speech is a fundamental part of being Word Smart. Why do people speak? They speak to communicate, inspire, persuade, lead, teach, and entertain. That's a whole lot of talking going on!

Think about how often you use speech throughout your day. You talk to your friends at school. You answer questions from your teachers. You may use speech to argue with your brother or sister about all sorts of things—or to teach your younger sister how to do a math problem. You might use speech to convince people to join causes or buy things for school fundraisers. These are all ways of being Word Smart.

You may have difficulty reading or writing but still be very Word Smart in the way that you speak. Many people who've been labeled *dyslexic* or *reading disabled* are actually wonderful storytellers, speakers, actors, comedians, or politicians. Some examples include actors Tom Cruise and Salma Hayek, comedians Whoopi Goldberg and Jay Leno, and singers Cher and John Lennon.

If you're a good speaker (and listener), you may be someone who others turn to when a speech needs to be made. You may be known as a good storyteller or the "class clown." Maybe you shine when doing oral reports. On the other hand, maybe getting up in front of a group of people or raising your hand in class scares you.

Did You Know?

You can have a stutter when you speak, but still be a great speaker, storyteller, or actor. Famous examples include Winston Churchill (leader of Britain in World War II), Nicholas Brendon (actor, Xander on *Buffy the Vampire Slayer*), and James Earl Jones (actor, the voice of Darth Vader in the *Star Wars* movies).

If you don't like speaking up, take some comfort from the fact that a lot of other people (grown-ups included) don't like to do it either. So, what's so hard about speaking? Many people don't like drawing attention to themselves. Or they worry that they will say something stupid.

If you're scared about speaking up in class:

* Do listen to what everyone else is saying in class.

* Do start speaking up more often. Try speaking up a little more each day. You don't have to do it all at once.

* Don't worry about what anyone else thinks when you talk.

If you're scared about an oral report or a presentation:

* Remember to breathe. It sounds obvious, but try it anyway. Breathing helps calm you down.

* Speak loudly, clearly, and slowly. You'll probably want to whisper, mumble, or rush—but if you do, you might have to do the speech over again.

> ## Did You Know?
> Martin Luther King Jr.'s famous "I Have a Dream" speech has been called one of the greatest pieces of *rhetoric,* or convincing speech, in the 20th century. Visit the National Civil Rights Museum on the Web to read the speech: *www.mecca.org/~crights/ dream.html*

* Practice in front of someone like a good friend or a parent. You'll get used to saying the words aloud and how it feels to make the presentation in front of an audience of one. This will make it easier to stand up in front of a bigger group.

* Highlight the important points in your report, so that you can find them easily when you're talking. If you practice enough, you may find you don't need your notes at all!

Speaking doesn't have to be scary. It can be as fun and simple as telling jokes or stories to your friends.

Telling jokes and stories is a good way to entertain people, but telling stories can also be very important. Storytellers have been valued members of cultures all over the world. Not only have they entertained their audiences, but they often have been the keepers of history and myth for their cultures. Family histories and religious traditions have been passed along for generations this way, too.

THE WRITTEN WORD

If you think about it, being able to read is one of the most amazing things in the world. These are just simple marks of ink on a page. How is it that you're able to find meaning in these marks? Look at the word *cat*. It's just three marks on the page, each one shaped in a different way. But when you read these marks, you probably begin to think about your own cat (if you have one) or about other cats that you've known or seen.

How is it that you can imagine all of this from just three simple marks? No one really knows. Somehow, in ways that scientists still don't fully understand, you're able look at these marks (and all the other marks on this page) and make sense of their meaning.

The ability to read opens up all kinds of doors into the world of knowledge and imagination. You can be sitting on your couch or at your desk in school and suddenly be transported to ancient Egypt, or to a rocket ship heading into outer space, or to a submarine deep under the sea. Reading a book is like entering a whole other world.

Did You Know?

Scientists tell us that people who use sign language—including the deaf and hearing impaired—are mostly using the Word Smart areas of the brain to communicate.

What kind of books do you most enjoy reading? Some people have favorite authors like R.L. Stine, J.K. Rowling, Walter Dean Myers, or Beverly Cleary and try to read all of their books. Other people favor certain *genres*, or categories of books, like mysteries, science fiction, westerns, romance, poetry, or plays. Some people love to read nonfiction books or magazines about animals, nature, history, cars, or space travel. And still others don't have any particular method for choosing books—they just read whatever they like.

There are different ways of reading books, and this knowledge can help you both inside and outside of school. You can read for pleasure or you can read for content. Sometimes you do both.

There are certain things that you *have* to read in school, like textbooks, handouts, and stories. Some of this material may really interest you, and some of it might not. When you're not as interested, you probably just want to read to get the information as quickly as you can. For these books and materials, reading for content is the key.

This kind of reading is called "inspectional reading." It may involve picking out key words and topic sentences (usually the first sentence of a paragraph). You also look at chapter headings and subheadings for other important phrases and pieces of information. Pictures and charts can also help you get at the basic meaning of the text.

Did You Know?

Reading for pleasure, or playful reading, is also called "ludic reading." Ludic (pronounced loo-dik) comes from the Latin word *ludere*, which means to play.

Reading can also be a pleasure and a treat. In order to really enjoy a book, try taking your time when you read. Read at your own pace, or even read more slowly and savor the words and the story. Give yourself permission to slow down and listen to the sounds of the words in your head, imagine the scenery, or think about the ideas in the book. Writers usually choose their words very carefully. Their word choices make a character's speech sound more real. Or they can create sound effects on the page (the splash of raindrops, the crackle of a fire, the whoosh of wind).

Try reading part of one of your favorite books out loud. What do the characters sound like? Do the words seem more funny or serious when read aloud? Try writing down responses to the story or to something a character says. Maybe you'll get an idea from reading and want to write a story of your own. Or maybe you'll want to draw the character, build a model of someplace in the book, or try acting out a scene. All of these ideas are ways to be Word Smart.

USING YOUR WORDS IN WRITING

The more you read, the more you may want to *write* to tell your own stories and express your own thoughts. People write in different ways. Some people hear what they want to write. Other people see things in their head and write to describe what they see. Some people use their feelings to help them write. Others find stories or poetry in the events and people around them and write about that.

What you may find when you start to write is that you have your own voice—something that makes the writing uniquely yours. Your voice can emerge whether you write poetry, stories, or even journal entries. This voice will come out of who you are and what you've done.

Don't worry about what your voice sounds like when you write or whether you have one. The most important thing to do when you write is to *write*. It's very easy to get put off of writing if you think that you won't be any good at it—even if it's something you really want to do. It's also very easy to get distracted by other things . . . so stop playing video games or sorting your socks, and try writing instead!

> ## Did You Know?
> The Nobel Prize–winning writer Saul Bellow said that he heard whole paragraphs with all the punctuation included! Poet Amy Lowell wrote that she doesn't hear a voice but that she feels a sense of words rather than actually hearing them.

It's okay to write about anything you want—even the first thing that crosses your mind. It doesn't matter if it's skateboarding, your big brother, math, or chocolate ice cream. Write about a topic for five minutes without stopping. (Don't worry about punctuation or spelling. You can always go back and fix those.)

After the five minutes are up, read what you've written. Some of it may be silly (and you probably stopped writing about chocolate ice cream at some point). But, most likely, there are some interesting words or phrases in your writing. Some of these may become the basis for a poem, story, or essay. This process is called *free writing*. Many writers do this to get started.

Here's another way to start writing: Stop whatever you're doing for a couple of minutes and just spend time thinking your thoughts. You don't have to think about anything in particular—whatever comes to mind is fine. After a couple of minutes, stop and consider what you "heard." Did you hear a voice in your head? Was the voice yours or someone else's? Were there actual words? Or did you mainly see pictures in your mind and have feelings? Start writing about it. Describe what the voice was saying, what the pictures looked like, or how you felt.

In the same way that actors may look at people around them for ideas, writers listen to the people around them. Becoming a better listener may give you ideas for poems or improve the dialogue (speech) in your stories. If you want to write but are really stuck for something to start writing about, there are a lot of books that have jumping-off points you can use.

OTHER WAYS OF BEING WORD SMART

As you can see, there are many ways to be Word Smart. You might show it by being a super speller or by having great grammar when you write. Or maybe spelling and grammar aren't your strong points, but you're able to write really creative stories with beautiful images in them.

You may love writing poetry but not enjoy writing book reports. You might like writing essays but not stories. You may enjoy practicing your handwriting, without paying much attention to the actual words you write. You may love writing, but not enjoy reading. Being Word Smart doesn't mean you have to love *every* aspect of words and their different uses. Each person is Word Smart in his or her own unique way.

Did You Know?

The most widely published mystery writer in the world—Agatha Christie—had problems with her spelling and grammar. There are over half a billion of her mystery books in print all over the world!

For example, you might be Word Smart through a love of single words. Maybe you like to collect favorite words, or look up words that you don't already know, or impress people with your knowledge of very long words. If any of these sound like you, then you could try some "word archeology."

EUREKA!

eu·re·ka \yŏo rē´kə\ *interj*
used to express triumph on discovery

You can "dig up" strange and difficult words and find out where they came from and how they've been used over the years. The longest and best dictionary for English is the *Oxford English Dictionary* or the *OED*. Because it's so big, the best place to find it is in the library. It includes just about all the words used in English. It gives a history for each word and explains its origins in other languages and how it developed step-by-step over time. The *OED* also gives examples of how word meanings (and spellings) change over the centuries.

Word archeology is fun and so is playing with the sounds of words. You could try tongue twisters, riddles, puns, or rhymes. Read nonsense poetry out loud or write your own. Try making up words that sound like what they represent—this is called *onomatopoeia*. You could even make up a secret language with your friends using words or hand gestures that only you understand!

Words can be fun—more than just vocabulary lists, spelling tests, or book reports that you have to do. Becoming more Word Smart doesn't have to be a chore. It can be a huge adventure.

Did You Know?

What's the longest word in the dictionary? It depends on how you look at it. One dictionary lists *supercalifragilisticexpialidocious* (from *Mary Poppins*). If you are willing to add diseases, then *pneunomoultramicroscopicsilicovolcanoconiosis* is the longest word. But if you count place names, then *Llanfairpwllgwyngyllgogerychwyrndrobwllllantysiliogogogoch* (the name of a village in Wales) is the longest word in the dictionary.

Fun Ways to Become More Word Smart

Here are some ways that you can expand and enjoy your Word Smart skills. Try *any* activity that appeals to you no matter how Word Smart you think you are.

1 **Write down your ideas as you get them.** Keep a little notebook (or miniature tape recorder) handy for putting down ideas that occur to you during the day.

2 **Read about what interests you.** Anything is fair game and everything counts: car magazines, art books, newspapers, science journals, comics, and more.

3 **Start a journal.** Write at least 250 words a day on any subject that you'd like. Write about your day, what you did in school, a book you're reading, what's happening in the world, or anything else that interests you.

4 **Start going to the library.** You can find a world of books and audio tapes there and they can be all yours—for free! All you have to do is sign up for a card. Librarians can help you find books on topics that interest you and recommend authors that you'd like. They can also make suggestions about books on tape you might enjoy.

5 **Look up words that you don't know in a dictionary.** Keep a list of words you come across that you don't know. If you keep doing this, you'll find that your vocabulary has gotten huge without your even noticing it!

6 **Have a regular storytelling time with your family.** The stories can be about anything you'd like: make up your own stories, retell favorite parts of books you've read and liked, or tell family stories.

7 **Make some important book lists.** Make a list of (1) your top ten favorite books of all time, (2) a list of books that you want to read over the next few months, and (3) a list of books that you want to make sure you read sometime during your life. Keep the lists handy to help direct your reading in the future.

8 **Play with words.** Do Mad Libs, crossword puzzles, Acrostics, find-a-words, anagrams, or other word puzzles that interest you. (Many daily newspapers have word games in their comics or entertainment sections.) Get together with friends and family to play games like Scrabble, Hangman, Anagrams, or Password.

9 **Play with spoken words.** Collect some of your favorite jokes, riddles, puns, tongue twisters, rhymes, long words, strange words, and other sounds of language and share them with friends, classmates, and family. And, if you'd like, make up some of your own!

10 **Join a book club where you can discuss books with others.** Local libraries are good places to go to do this and may have clubs that focus on kids' books, mysteries, science fiction, or the classics. If you can't find a book club, try starting your own with your family or friends.

11 **Write your favorite authors.** Look up the email or mailing address of writers who you enjoy reading, and write to them with questions about their books, how they got started writing, or anything else that you're curious about.

12 **Go listen to a writer speak.** Writers often make appearances at bookstores, libraries, local colleges, and other places within the community to read from their work and answer questions from fans. Go hear a poet, novelist, children's author, or other writer speak or read from his or her books.

13 **Learn another language.** It can be Spanish, German, Chinese, or any other language that interests you. Learning other languages is another way to be Word Smart. (Learning English as a second language makes you Word Smart, too!) You may be able to find language courses at your school, but if there aren't any, check at your community center or library for resources.

14 **Keep a writer's journal.** Use this journal to record your own poems, stories, or plays. You could even add favorite quotes, passages, and dialogue from your reading or from things that you overhear other people say. Many famous writers have kept their own journals in this or a similar way.

15 **Attend a play.** Many plays are put on in local schools and by community theater groups. (If you can, try attending a Shakespeare play. He was one of the most incredibly Word Smart writers who ever lived and his 37 plays and 154 sonnets are still widely read and admired today even though they were written 400 years ago.)

16 **If you like discussing ideas, join your school's debate team (if it has one).** If your school doesn't have a debate team, ask your teachers if debates can be staged in any of your classes. Debating can be a great way to sharpen not only your speaking skills, but also your skills in logic and research. It's also a great way to learn about different subjects since you could be asked to debate topics from science, health, history, social studies, or English.

What If Word Smart Isn't Speaking Your Language?

Remember, each person is Word Smart in some way. But you might find some Word Smart activities frustrating to do or hard to understand if your strengths are in other areas. For example, if you're a Picture Smart person, reading or writing could be harder for you because you might view letters as parts of pictures, rather than as parts of words. Because you may be used to viewing things in your head from different angles, you may spin letters around (like b's and d's) and confuse them in the words you're reading. Or, if you're Body Smart, you may get frustrated by having to sit still when you read and write. You may prefer to learn while moving around or to learn in ways that involve more touch or "hands on" work.

You can always use the smarts you're strongest or most comfortable in to become more Word Smart.

Here are seven ways to do it:

 If you're Music Smart: Read aloud and listen to the sounds of the words. Read silly poetry by people like Shel Silverstein, Ogden Nash, and Lewis Carroll, because they played with sounds and words. Try singing or rapping your spelling list or facts that you're memorizing (that way if you forget during a test you can hum the answer very quietly back to yourself). Use music as a jumping off point for writing. Write about what you hear and what it makes you think about.

 If you're Logic Smart: Use a computer word processing software program when you write. Check your spelling, punctuation, and grammar on your own first. *Then* run the spelling and grammar check to see if you missed anything. Checking your work first will help you learn more from any mistakes the checker finds.

 If you're Picture Smart: Close your eyes and picture what you read. For example, if you're reading a story that you're having a hard time understanding, shut your eyes and picture the scene, the characters, and the action in the story. Illustrations and pictures can help guide you through your reading, too.

 If you're Body Smart: Physically play with words and letters. There are many magnetic word kits you can buy. Or you can make your own with paper and magnets that have adhesive on one side (try looking in an office supply store for these). Put the paper on the sticky side of the magnet and cut the magnet into a different shape or size if you'd like. Using a steel surface, practice your spelling, write poetry, or tell stories.

 If you're People Smart: Talk about what you're reading with your friends or family. Form a study group to study spelling or vocabulary words. Working and studying with others can help you learn better.

 If you're Self Smart: Start keeping a journal of what you're think-ing and feeling. Every time you write in the journal, you'll be improving your writing, spelling, and grammar through practice. Think about what you're learning in school—how does the book you're reading in class make you feel? Use this as a way to connect who you are and how you feel to what you're learning in school.

 If you're Nature Smart: When you're reading a book or magazine, think about what kinds of animals and plants are in it. Write descriptions of the natural scenes you see, or take notes about leaves or rocks you collect. You might even find you prefer reading outside.

A lot of school involves being Word Smart. In almost every class you'll be asked to read, write, present a report, or just participate in class discussions. So being Word Smart can help you do better in school. Use some of the suggestions above to help you develop this intelligence. When you have chances in school to use your strengths and interests in Word Smart activities, take them! Use your Picture Smart skills to draw pictures for a presentation in class. Or use your People Smart skills to referee a class debate. Or use your Nature Smart observation abilities to gather material for a report. There are more ways to develop Word Smart than you might think.

If you ever find yourself hating words because you have to . . .

* take a hard test full of words you don't know

* read a boring book

* give a speech to a group and you're scared to do it

* write a book report and you can't think of anything to say

. . . just remember how amazing it is that you can do these things in the first place. Remember that these marks on the page and these speech sounds in the air are truly magic. And congratulate yourself for all the Word Smart abilities that you already possess.

What If You're a Word Smart Whiz?

If you're already very Word Smart, that's great! But guess what? You can still become *even more* Word Smart. Use your reading to work on your speaking, or your speaking to build up your writing. There are always new ways to learn and grow.

Your Word Smart skills can help you build your other intelligences. Here are some Word Smart ideas you can use to help you understand and develop the other intelligences in school and in life.

 For Music Smart, write your own words and rhymes to songs to help you learn melodies and rhythm.

 For Logic Smart, talk yourself through problems. For example, if you're doing a math problem, talk quietly to yourself about how to solve the problem: "Let's see, first I have to divide, then multiply, then…." If you're having trouble with a math problem or science experiment, also try making it into a word problem.

 For Picture Smart, when you're reading, picture what the characters and the places look like. If it helps, draw a scene, map, or even a character. This may help you understand a complicated book, or it might just be something that you enjoy doing whenever you read.

 For Body Smart, act in school plays or in skits that you and your friends put together. Imagine how the character you're playing walks, sits, even sneezes! Then try to move in the same way.

 For People Smart, watch the people around you. A key to being a good speaker or storyteller is convincing people. To do that, it helps to understand why people do what they do and be good at reading people's responses.

For Self Smart, keep a personal journal. Use it to look at your feelings, explore your goals, and examine your responses to the people and events around you.

 For Nature Smart, take a page from many other cultures over the ages and write myths to explain what you see in nature and all around you. Why don't cats and dogs get along anyway? How did the stars get in the sky? Why is grass green?

Look to the Future

What can you do with your Word Smart skills when you get older? A lot of very different things. Some of the careers you might look into include:

 advertising or marketing copy writer ▪ advocate ▪ archivist ▪ editor ▪ English teacher (or any kind of teacher) ▪ grant writer ▪ indexer ▪ information scientist (someone who uses technology to manage and use information) ▪ journalist ▪ lawyer ▪ librarian ▪ lobbyist ▪ museum curator ▪ paralegal ▪ poet ▪ politician ▪ professional public speaker ▪ proofreader ▪ publicist/public relations specialist ▪ radio or television announcer ▪ researcher ▪ screenwriter ▪ speech pathologist ▪ speech writer ▪ storyteller ▪ translator ▪ Web editor ▪ writer ▪ and many more!

Get Smart with These Resources

 ## Books and Magazines

The Kids' Magnetic Poetry Book and Creativity Kit by Dave Kapell and Sally Steenland (New York: Workman, 1998). Explores the joys of writing poetry with games for groups, writing jump-offs, and a visit to the poet's toolbox (which teaches some classic forms of poetry).

Mad Libs Series by Price, Roger, and Leonard Stern (New York: Price, Stern, and Sloan, 1974–2002). This word game can be played with a friend or with a group. Helps develop grammar skills, vocabulary, and a silly sense of humor.

Stone Soup
P.O. Box 83 • Santa Cruz, CA 95063 • 1-800-447-4569
www.stonesoup.com
A well-respected literary magazine written and illustrated by and for young writers and artists. Filled with short stories, poetry, reviews, and illustrations, it is published six times a year.

The Young Writer's Companion by Sarah Ellis (Toronto: Groundwood Books, 1999). If you want to write, this book will help you explore the joys of words, wordplay, writing, famous writers, and creative "fooling around" with language.

The Young Writer's Guide to Getting Published by Kathy Henderson (Cincinnati, OH: Writers Digest Books, 2001). An excellent resource and reference book for young aspiring writers. Includes over 100 publications and contests, writing tips, how to prepare your manuscript for submission, and profiles of professional editors and young writers.

 ## Organizations

The Children's Book Council
12 W. 37th Street, 2nd floor
New York, NY 10018-7480
(212) 966-1990
www.cbcbooks.org/html/links.html
Write or email some of your favorite children's book authors and illustrators by visiting this list of links to their contact information and often their homepages.

Scripps Howard National Spelling Bee
312 Walnut Street, 28th Floor
Cincinnati, OH 45202
www.spellingbee.com
Visit Carolyn's Corner on this Web site for information specifically for participants.
She updates the information weekly and is a rich source of bee information, study tips,
activities, and word history.

 Other

"Language Families of the World"
www.exploratoriumstore.com/chartsposters.html
A colorful, fact-filled, and up-to-date chart designed by Stanford linguists for the
Exploratorium. Trace the history of the English language, find out what the top 12 languages in the world are, or learn about languages you've never heard of before.

Magnetic Poetry
P.O. Box 14862 • Minneapolis, MN 55414 • 1-800-370-7697
www.magneticpoetry.com
Any steel surface can become a verbal playground. There are kits for kids or start with
the basic set (with over 400 words). Spark your creativity and improve your writing. If
you like learning different languages, the kits also come in French, Spanish, German,
and American Sign Language.

 Web Sites

Arrak Anagrams
www.arrak.fi/ag/index_en.html
Whether you're stuck solving an anagram or you're trying to create new ones, this site
can help you. Type in jumbled letters or even your own name, and the site will rearrange
the letters to form a new word or phrase.

Chapter 2

Music Smart

Quick Quiz

Do you:

* enjoy singing?
* like listening to music?
* play an instrument?
* read music?
* remember melodies or tunes easily?
* easily recognize many different songs?
* hear the differences between different instruments being played together?
* hum or sing while thinking or doing tasks?
* easily pick up rhythms in the sounds around you?
* like making musical sounds with your body (humming, clapping your hands, snapping your fingers, or tapping your feet)?
* make up or write your own songs or raps?
* remember facts by making up a song for them?

If you answered yes to any of the questions above, then you just identified some of the ways you're Music Smart!

What Does It Mean
to Be Music Smart?

For a start, if you're Music Smart, you *really* like music. You appreciate and hear rhythm, melody, and different patterns in music. You may be able to tell whether music is being played or sung in tune, what the notes or chords in a song are, or what different instruments in a piece sound like. You may be curious about and appreciate many different kinds of music. Most likely, you enjoy activities like singing, playing music, listening to CDs, or attending concerts. You may show this type of intelligence by writing your own songs, playing an instrument (or maybe many instruments), making (or improvising) your own instruments, or singing on key. Or you may show it by hearing music in the sounds of daily life (like the melody in a birdsong or a catchy rhythm in the sounds of a train moving on railroad tracks). You can probably tell that there's a lot that goes into making music and being Music Smart—maybe more than you ever thought.

Our culture doesn't put such a great importance on being smart with music. Many people think it's a nice *talent* to have on the side but don't consider it to be an *intelligence.* Everybody isn't expected to be musical in modern society in the same way that everybody is expected to be able to read and write. In school, for example, you probably won't be required to pass a music test to go on to the next grade, but you *are* expected to pass tests in reading, writing, and math.

On the whole, only a few people in our culture are thought to be really musical: concert violinists, rock stars, jazz artists, rap groups, and pop singers, to name just a few members of this special group. Other people aren't really expected to develop their Music Smart abilities, except to enjoy listening to music or seeing performers in concert (or on TV), or to play music at home, in extracurricular groups in the community, or in groups at school.

Yet even in school, if there's a problem with the budget, musical activities such as band, orchestra, or chorus are among the first programs to be cut. They certainly aren't going to take out the reading or math programs first! As a result, if you don't come from a musical family or have access to music in school or through a community center, it's very likely that you haven't had opportunities to learn and grow musically.

In many cultures, however, music plays an active role in daily life. In Hungary, kids like you study music and music theory in school every day (this helps them learn more in school overall). In Japan, children as young as the age of three start learning to play the violin or piano through the "Suzuki method." In Senegal, *griots,* or "news-singers," still deliver the news and keep the local history.

All over the world, and for most of human history, music has been a *key way* in which knowledge has been passed from one generation to the next. Before there were books to store information, people had to store things in their minds. Older generations taught this information to younger people who would then carry that knowledge inside of them until they, too, became old. Sometimes this meant remembering thousands of family names from the past, or thousands of plants and herbal remedies, or the entire history of a tribe. Tribespeople in Africa, singers in Turkey and Eastern Europe, and medieval monks all stored and shared information this way.

These people were like walking libraries! One of the reasons they were able to remember so much was because they put the information in a *musical* format: They chanted it rhythmically, sang it as a part of regular tribal rituals, or wrote epic songs (long, involved story songs) that contained this important information. (You'll find out later in the chapter how music can help you learn and remember things, too.) Some stories that you may be familiar with, like Greek myths and stories from the Bible, were passed down this way. They were sung or chanted before they were finally written down.

> ## Did You Know?
>
> In Papua New Guinea in the south Pacific Ocean, educated members of the Iatmul people know between 10,000 and 20,000 clan names from memory and without having anything written down. The clan names are learned through rhythmic chanting.

Music continues to be very important to many people around the world, where in some parts, you have to be musically intelligent to function in everyday life. Why is music still so important to so many people? It's a part of who they are. Music is used to communicate, learn, share, and have fun. You can use music for all of these things in your own life. For these reasons and many others, it's worth learning more about the different ways to be Music Smart.

What can being Music Smart do for you?

* It can help you learn more in school and remember important things.
* You can use it to communicate in different ways.
* It can bring you pleasure.

Things you may do every day that use this intelligence:

listen to music ▪ play an instrument (any instrument) ▪ sing (in a choir or even along to the radio) ▪ write songs ▪ play in your own band or music group ▪ hum, sing, or tap while you work or think

DEVELOPING AN EAR FOR MUSIC

Some people don't sing or play an instrument, but they still love to *listen* to their favorite music. There's more to listening to music than just hearing the sounds. *Listening* to music—not just hearing it—is a key part of developing Music Smart skills. When you listen to music, you can hear the melodies, rhythms, and tones. You can tune in to different patterns and even structures in the music. You also can notice what the different instruments sound like and how they're used in the song.

One way to understand music better is to think about what you're listening to and ask yourself questions about it. Do you think that the music is intended to make you feel a certain way? How do the words, or lyrics (if there are any), work with the music? Is the music (not just the lyrics) telling a story? Does the music remind you of other songs or pieces of music? Why? How good are the musicians? What do you think they bring to the music? All of these things, and more, are a part of *actively* listening to music.

Think about your favorite songs, groups, and kinds of music. There are a lot of different kinds of music to like: rock, jazz, rap, heavy metal, reggae, gospel, blues, classical, country, world music, folk, dance, techno, and pop to name just a few. Have you heard each of these different kinds of music? Do you want to? Why or why not? What are your favorite kinds of music? Who are some of your favorite musicians, singers, or groups? Why do you like them? Every musical artist shows his or her own unique brand of musical intelligence. But so do you, because you have the ability to understand and enjoy different aspects of the artist's songs and music.

Did You Know?

If you were growing up among the Anang of northern Nigeria, by the time you were five years old you'd be expected to know hundreds of songs. Songs are an important way of communicating information among tribal members. There are songs for work, play, war, marriage, and business. Anyone who doesn't know the songs would have a hard time knowing what was going on in the community.

Listening to and understanding music isn't just thinking about it or analyzing it. Part of listening is how the music makes you feel. Songwriters and composers often write music with an emotion in mind. It may be how they feel when they're creating the musical piece, or it may be an emotion they want to get across to whoever listens to it. And of course, when you listen, you bring your own emotions and experiences to the song.

Some people use music to lift their mood or to calm themselves down. Others listen to music to inspire them. Notice how different types of

Did You Know?

Certain types of classical music, especially Baroque music, are good to listen to while you study, because it is thought that they improve concentration and memory. Some teachers even use this music in their classrooms to help their students learn more and study better.

music make you feel. What type of music makes you feel happy, energetic, sad, angry, focused, friendly, reflective, relaxed, or imaginative?

Other people listen to music to help them learn and remember more when they study. There are many ways to use music to learn and remember things. (Find out ways to do this in the tips later in the chapter.) But maybe you like to listen to music for the simplest (and perhaps best) reason of all—because you love it!

MAKING MUSIC

Singing and playing musical instruments may be the first things that come to mind when you think about being Music Smart. When you sing along to the radio or in a choir, you're being Music Smart. When you play trombone in the school band or improvise percussion instruments with things on your desk, you're being Music Smart. You can make music anywhere you go. Maybe you sing while taking out the trash and tap your feet while doing math problems. Making music—no matter how you do it—is a way of being Music Smart.

If you've never tried to play an instrument or sing, don't assume you can't. You might feel more comfortable singing by yourself or teaching yourself how to play an instrument like the guitar or piano. Or you might think about joining a school band or choir, where everyone is learning something new. If you have the opportunity, you could also look into taking private lessons from a music teacher.

Learning to make music uses your other intelligences, too. As you learn to count out the music and recognize the structure and patterns in a musical piece, you might find that your Logic Smart skills are getting a workout. Or you might develop your Body Smart abilities by being more aware of your breathing and posture when you sing, or by improving your motor skills and coordination when you play a musical instrument like a cello or clarinet.

Playing an instrument or singing is more than being able to read music or sing on key. Making music is also about expression and feeling. Just as listening to music can make you feel certain ways, playing music can, too. You can cheer yourself up by playing a piece of ragtime on the piano or make yourself sad or thoughtful by playing a slow air on the violin. Working through an especially hard section in a piece of music can leave you with a feeling of accomplishment and pride—and it should!

Playing and singing music written by other people also can give you insight into the songwriter's feelings. Understanding what feeling the songwriter or composer was trying to communicate can let you explore your own feelings, too. (This is a good way to explore how you're Self Smart!) This is true whether you're playing a Bach concerto or a song by jazz great Billie Holiday. You might find that how the song makes you feel is different than how the songwriter or composer intended. This might lead you to play the song differently so it reflects more of your own feelings.

Did You Know?

Musical intelligence is probably the first intelligence to appear. Babies respond and move to music long before they start talking. Prodigies, or children who are *very* talented *very* young, are also pretty common in music. Award-winning cellist Yo-Yo Ma played his first public concert at the age of 6!

Playing music with (and for) other people can make you feel good, too. It's a way of sharing the feelings in the music and making them larger and more intense. It also builds bonds with others and gives you a sense of community—whether you sing with a parent while cooking dinner, join a church choir, or start a garage band with your friends.

So, when you make music, you're doing more than you realize. You may be thinking, expressing feelings, solving problems, making friends, and growing and sharing an important part of yourself.

WRITING MUSIC

Many people share ideas and feelings through writing music, which they might perform or let other people play. Composing, or writing, your own songs is another way to be Music Smart. Whether you noodle on the piano, write formal pieces on your violin, or pull together songs in a band, you're writing music.

Composing a piece of music or writing a song doesn't have to be a big or formal deal. The song can be as simple or as complicated as you'd like. Writing music is basically about creating patterns of tones, notes, or rhythms that you like and playing around with them. Find some sounds or noises that you enjoy and let them inspire you. Maybe you'll find a catchy rhythm in some construction noise or the sound of a washing machine and set a rap to it. Maybe the sounds of a storm inspire you to create a piece on the piano that sounds like raindrops coming down.

> ## Did You Know?
>
> American composer George Gershwin once said, "I frequently hear music in the heart of noise." He got many of his best musical ideas from the sounds of the city: jackhammers on the city streets, the sounds of machines in factories, and cars on busy streets.

Perhaps you hear more music in your head than you do in the world around you. Can you make that music in your head come alive? Hum or sing the tune or notes if you don't have words. Tap on an upended bucket to create a beat. Strum on a guitar until you find a chord that sounds right. No matter how you start writing a song, give yourself time to fool around and play. Remember, you're writing the song only for yourself at this point. Play the notes and make the noises that sound right to you.

You may want to share your music with other people. You might want to start by playing for family and friends. If you enjoy that, you may decide to branch out and play your music for lots of people. You might be able to play your music in school. If you do want to perform your music in public, start looking in your community for talent shows and open mike (microphone) nights in coffeehouses and cafes. You may find a whole community of people who like to write and play their own music. What a great way to explore your Music Smart skills!

GETTING IN TUNE WITH YOUR MUSICAL MIND

You might be interested to know that your Music Smart mind is at work even when you're not thinking about or listening to music. Your musical mind is part of your everyday life. Start looking for your musical mind at work in school. You might notice that you're tapping rhythmically on the desk or humming quietly under your breath as you're reading a book, working on a math problem, or studying Spanish vocabulary words. That's your musical mind helping you process ideas and information.

Playing music, as well as listening to it, can help you focus your thoughts. Music can help you create art and inventions, brainstorm ideas, and solve problems. Many scientists, writers, and artists have used music to help them learn, think through problems, and get inspired. Albert Einstein played the violin while he mulled over physics problems. Novelist Stephen King listens to heavy metal when he's writing his books. In the 1950s, writers from the Beat Movement like Jack Kerouac and Allen Ginsburg were inspired by the sounds and rhythms of jazz. They tried to create those same sounds and rhythms, or beats, in the language of their poetry and stories. Artists Henri Matisse and Jackson Pollock also used jazz to guide them to new ideas and ways for making their art.

Did You Know?

Some people get paid to make funny noises. Foley artists create all of the sounds behind a movie except for gunshots and explosions. All footsteps, eating noises, doors slamming, or slimy alien noises are the work of a foley artist. Foley artists use and do almost anything to make the right noises for a movie— including licking their own arms (for kissing noises)!

Sometimes your musical mind is triggered by the sounds around you: the gurgle of water in a fountain, the leaves blowing in the wind, the peck-peck-peck of a woodpecker on a tree, or the booming of thunder during a storm. Cities also make "music" with the sounds of honking horns, subways, sirens, and people walking and talking. The world is full of music, and songwriters and composers use these sounds in their own songs and pieces.

Writers can also draw on the sounds and music of life. Have you ever read any books by Dr. Seuss? If you have, remember how rhythmic and almost musical the words are in stories like *The Cat in the Hat* or *Green Eggs and Ham*? Dr. Seuss said that the rhythms for his rhymes first came to him when he was riding on a train and started listening to the clackity-clack of the wheels on the tracks beneath him.

When you were reading just now, could you almost hear the train wheels or the city noises? Did you know that you can play music and sounds in your head? You've probably pictured, or visualized, things in your mind before. Well, you can do the same thing with sounds and music. It's called *musical imagery,* and it involves hearing music with your mind instead of with your ears.

If you'd like to see how good you are at musical imagery, try some of the sound and music ideas below. Listen to each of these pieces *in your mind only* (no fair humming or singing the tune out loud). If you'd like to make it a little more fun or challenging, you can experiment with altering the sounds. Some ideas for changing the sounds are in parentheses.

* The Happy Birthday Song (played on a kazoo)
* Your favorite song (sung by your family)
* A song or jingle from a commercial (played much too fast)
* The patter of rain on the roof (instead of rain, make it rocks)
* The sound of opening a pop-top can of soda (one that's been shaken up a lot!)

How did you do? Were some of the sounds more difficult to hear than others? Just like picturing things in your head, you might find musical imagery easy and fun or you might find it hard to do. That's okay—everybody's different. Practice using musical imagery. You might find that you start to listen to music more carefully and that your musical memory improves. (You might also improve your memory as a whole, if you tend to remember things to music.)

If you found the list of musical images easy to hear, then it's almost like you have an "inner CD player" that you can turn on any time you like—while you're studying, washing dishes, or cleaning up. It certainly does help the time go faster, doesn't it?

Fun Ways to Become More Music Smart

Here are some ways that you can expand and enjoy your Music Smart skills. Try *any* activity that appeals to you no matter how Music Smart you think you are.

1 **Listen to as many different kinds of music as you can.** Regularly listen to a variety of different musical styles on the radio (for example, blues, jazz, classical, country and western, popular, rap, gospel). Don't automatically assume that you hate a certain type of music. Give it a chance—you might be surprised at how much you like music you don't normally listen to.

2 **Listen to music from different parts of the world.** Try listening to music from Ireland, Mexico, India, China, or anyplace else that you're curious about. In some communities, you can find this music on the radio (especially on public radio stations) or in the library. You can also go online and listen to radio stations and music from around the world. (Type the words "world music" into a search engine to help you find music to listen to.)

3 **Sing with your family or friends.** Sing your favorite songs or learn new ones from each other. Making music with other people can be a lot of fun, so have sing-a-longs with your family on a regular basis. Or get some simple percussion instruments (for example, a drum, castanets, cymbals, a tambourine) and play them as background to some of your favorite recorded music.

4 **Play musical games with family or friends.** For example, play "Name That Tune" where you sing a few bars of a song and everyone else has to guess what the song is.

5 **Go to see live music whenever you get the chance.** There is often free music or concerts at fairs, parks, festivals, and local colleges. You might also check out recitals, auditions, and play rehearsals.

6 **Get involved in music at your school.** If your school has a choir, a band, or an orchestra, go for it. You'll learn to read music, you may have the opportunity to try different instruments, and you'll get to know a bunch of other people who are as curious about music as you are.

7 **Create or improvise instruments with whatever you have around your home.** The kitchen is a good place to scavenge for things to make instruments—pots and pans, glasses with different levels of water in them, wooden spoons, and silverware. Make a homemade maraca by filling a plastic container with dried beans, tacks, paperclips, or pebbles.

8 **Learn to read music.** This is often a part of school music programs like band, choir, or orchestra. There also is software that can help you do this.

9 **Promote music in your school and community.** If your school doesn't have a music program, talk to your teachers or your principal about how music can be brought into the classroom. Be the "squeaky wheel" that helps bring music into your school.

10 **Sit down with a friend and listen to a piece of music carefully.** Listen to as many different elements as you can, such as the instruments or the use of melody, rhythm, tone, and timbre (the resonance of the instruments). Can you identify those different elements? Do you hear any musical patterns in the music? How good is the performance? Is there anything else that the music is "saying" to you? Talk with each other about what you hear. Did you hear the same things?

11 **If you have the opportunity, take private music lessons on your favorite instrument.** Private lessons are sometimes available through local community centers and education programs. If you're unable to get private lessons, try teaching yourself to play piano, guitar, or harmonica using a computer software program or a book.

12 **Become more aware of the music around you.** Start by taking a few minutes to listen to the music and rhythms of nature, or to the rhythms in the busy world of traffic, people, and machines. Then write a piece of music using whatever instrument you'd like—your voice, a piano, a guitar, or anything else (even slapping rhythms on a table).

13 **Compose a song or musical piece.** Try using composition software to create your own music. Inexpensive computer software programs that give you the ability to combine many different instruments in a piece are now available. These programs will even print out the music you've written in musical notation. (Just a few years ago, only professional music studios had this kind of software.)

14 **Start a band.** Get together with a group of friends and create your own rock band, rap group, a cappella choir, or other musical combo. Then perform at school or in your neighborhood. Who knows? You might be on your way to stardom! (Even if you don't make it to the top, you'll still have a good time.)

What If Music Smart Isn't "Playing Your Song"?

You might wonder what all this has to do with you if you are doubting your Music Smart abilities. The shortest answer is: Music can help you learn more in school and feel better overall. Even if you *think* you sing so badly that dogs howl or you can't pick up an instrument without breaking it, don't believe it. You *are* Music Smart and you *can* develop this intelligence.

You might already be using Music Smart skills without realizing it. Humming while you fix something or solve brainteasers is one way. Using music to spur your story writing or drawing is another. Dancing is another way of showing off your Music Smart abilities. (Dancing is a good example of how the different intelligences work together—you're using your Music Smart, Body Smart, and even Picture Smart skills when you dance.)

Remember there are many ways of being Music Smart. Even if you can't sing on key, you can still learn how to play an instrument. It may help to find a good music teacher—a friend, a private teacher, or one at school—someone you feel comfortable with and who will encourage you each step of the way. As you learn to play an instrument, or to play one better, be patient with yourself. No one learns these things overnight, and everyone, even someone who's super musical, has to practice, practice, practice in order to improve. After awhile you'll start to find some real joy and satisfaction in expressing the music that's inside of you.

If you don't want to make music, you can still enjoy music by listening to it and understanding it. *Anyone* can become more Music Smart. You can always use the smarts you're strongest or most comfortable in to become more Music Smart.

Here are seven ways to do it:

 If you're Word Smart: Listen to the lyrics of songs. Pay attention to how the lyrics work with the music. Does the song tell a story? If it does tell a story, is it through the lyrics, the music, or both together? Does the plot of the story develop throughout the piece of music?

 If you're Logic Smart: Find the math in music. Part of music is about patterns and counting. Look for repeating patterns and themes and notice how they help structure the music. Most music has a time signature and musicians have to learn how to count out the music so that they're all playing at the same speed. Learn how to count out music and see if you can figure out the different time signatures of pieces you listen to.

 If you're Picture Smart: Draw, paint, or sculpt what you hear. Perhaps the music inspires actual images for you. Or maybe you'll see a flow of colors or shapes. Try designing a brand new kind of musical instrument and imagine what it would sound like—you might even want to build it!

 If you're Body Smart: Move to the music. Dancing is a good place to start, but any kind of movement—aerobics, yoga, tai chi, or even doing beadwork and jewelry-making or building models— can be done to music. If you like building or making things, create your own musical instrument from materials you find around your home.

If you're People Smart: Try making music with other people. Sing songs with your friends or family. Or if you'd prefer, use simple instruments like spoons, boxes, and glasses to have a rhythmic jam session.

 If you're Self Smart: Pick out different kinds of music and listen to it. What does the music make you feel and think about? What is it about the music that makes you feel that way? Is the melody cheerful or sad? Is the tempo upbeat or is it slow? Do the sounds of the different instruments change your mood? Listen to a piece of music and then write or draw what you feel.

 If you're Nature Smart: Listen for sounds in music that remind you of sounds found in nature—birdsong, gurgling water, rising wind. Listen to music about nature or animals. For example, Tchaikovsky's "Peter and the Wolf" is based on a Russian folktale and features many animal characters. Each animal in the piece is represented by a different instrument. There are also CDs and tapes that combine music and nature sounds—water, whale songs, forest noises—that you might enjoy.

What If You're a Music Smart Maestro?

Even if you're "in tune" with your Music Smart abilities, you can still expand and develop them even more. If you really like listening to music, try playing an instrument. Learn how to read music. If you already play an instrument, you might start taking more advanced lessons. Or you might want to try a different instrument to see if you enjoy it as much as the one you play now—or even more! Try composing your own songs and playing them for people. If you're used to playing solo, join a group at school or in your community. If you can't find one to join, start your own.

Your Music Smart skills can help you build your other intelligences. Here are some Music Smart ideas you can use to help you understand and develop the other intelligences in school and in life.

 For Word Smart, set spelling words and vocabulary to music. Remember how you learned your ABCs to a song when you were much younger? Well, the same thing can work for you now, whether you're learning new words, remembering dates in history, or memorizing the names of countries or states. Notice the music and sounds that take place in a story or book you're reading. For example, if there's a thunderstorm going on in the story, take a moment to actually listen to the sounds of the storm in your mind's ear.

 For Logic Smart, set math to music. Have you ever heard the song "Multiplication Rock"? It explains how multiplication works and makes it easy to remember. You can set any kind of math facts to music. Whether it's multiplication tables or measurements, music can make the facts a lot easier to learn and remember.

 For Picture Smart, play different types of recorded music and see what kinds of visual images, feelings, or ideas come to you while you listen. It may be the faces of people you know, buildings, basic shapes, or simply colors. Try creating a collage of images based on your favorite song.

 For Body Smart, try moving to the music. Move any way you want to, it doesn't have to be dancing. (You don't have to do it where anybody can see you.) Be as silly or as serious as the music makes you feel. Be aware of what your body is doing. Are you tapping your toes, nodding your head, or moving your hips to the rhythm?

 For People Smart, use music as a way to reach out to people. If you normally play music by yourself, make music with other people and see how it feels. Go to concerts and watch how other people enjoy music. Volunteer to be an usher or to hand out programs at local music events.

 For Self Smart, listen to music and songs that you used to love. Have your musical tastes changed? Do the same songs mean different things to you now? When music makes you feel something, notice what the emotion is. Create a collection of your favorite pieces of music on tape or CD that influence your mood—make a happy music mix or maybe a relaxing one.

 For Nature Smart, listen for music in nature. Go outside and listen for melodies in birdsongs or rhythms in the flow of traffic. Do certain kinds of animals, insects, or sounds in nature remind you of particular instruments? What about the sounds of the city? Do you hear instruments or music there?

Look to the Future

So, what can you do with your Music Smart when you get older? A lot of very different things. Some of the careers you might look into include:

 acoustician ▪ composer ▪ choral director ▪ conductor ▪ disc jockey ▪ ethnomusicologist ▪ foley artist ▪ instrument maker ▪ jingle writer ▪ lyricist ▪ music arranger ▪ music copyist ▪ music director/ supervisor ▪ music editor (film and video) ▪ music librarian ▪ music producer ▪ music researcher ▪ music teacher ▪ music therapist ▪ musician ▪ piano tuner ▪ singer ▪ songwriter ▪ sound effects editor for movies ▪ sound engineer (for recording studios; film, radio, and TV; live music and performances) ▪ studio director or manager ▪ video/film sound designer ▪ and many more!

Get Smart with These Resources

 Books

Country & Blues Guitar for the Musically Hopeless by Carol McComb and Barry Geller (Palo Alto, CA: Klutz, 1988). Ignore the title, and enjoy teaching yourself how to play guitar no matter what your musical skills may be.

Country & Blues Harmonica for the Musically Hopeless by John Gindick (Palo Alto, CA: Klutz, 1984). You don't have to be musically hopeless to use this book, regardless of the title. Teach yourself how to play harmonica and let the fun begin.

Jazz: An American Saga by James Lincoln Collier (New York: Henry Holt and Company, 1997). This is a fun, enthusiastic, and accessible crash course in a uniquely American musical form. Covers its history, its many forms from traditional bebop to modern fusion, and contains an excellent list of key recordings to follow up with.

One Love, One Heart: A History of Reggae by James Haskins (New York: Jump at the Sun/Hyperion, 2001). Tracing reggae's history from its African roots to its political and danceable present.

So, You Wanna Be a Rock Star? How to Create Music, Get Gigs, and Maybe Even Make It Big by Stephen Anderson (Hillsboro, OR: Beyond Words Publishing, 1999). This guide takes you through breaking into the music industry, choosing the right instrument for you, planning budgets, putting together a band, rehearsing, getting gigs, and more.

A Young Person's Guide to Music by Neil Ardley (New York: Dorling Kindersley Publishing, Inc., 2000). Find out everything you ever wanted to know about music—how the different sounds are made, how the instruments are made and played, how different instruments were invented, and the appeal of percussion.

The Young Person's Guide to Orchestra by Anita Ganeri (Orlando, FL: Harcourt Brace, 1996). Get an overview of an entire orchestra and then learn how different instruments make their unique sounds. Includes a CD of classical music and history.

 Music

World Playground: A Musical Adventure for Kids (Putumayo). With songs from Chile, Australia, Jamaica, Greece, Senegal, and many other places, this award-winning, upbeat compilation of World music is designed to introduce you to music and cultures from around the world and even in your own backyard.

World Playground 2 (Putumayo). This sequel spans the musical globe like the original, with musical stops in Colombia, Trinidad and Tobago, India, the Basque region (in Spain), Algeria, and many other countries.

 **Software**

Music Ace and Music Ace 2

Harmonic Vision, Inc. • 155 North Wacker Drive, Suite 725 • Chicago, IL 60606 •
1-800-474-0903 • *www.harmonicvision.com*

An award-winning software package designed for kids to learn music notation, music theory, and compose music on a "doodle pad."

Voyetra

Voyetra Turtle Beach • 5 Odell Plaza • Yonkers, NY 10701 • 1-800-233-9377 •
www.voyetra.com

Music software designed to make it easy to create, learn, and make music. Also has software to teach you how to play the guitar (Teach Me Guitar) and the piano (Teach Me Piano).

 Web Sites

Berklee College of Music

www.berklee.edu/careers

This lists a wide variety of careers in music and sound and has helpful descriptions of the different kinds of jobs. Also includes links to music-related associations and a detailed resource list.

Chapter 3

Logic Smart

Quick Quiz

Do you:

* find numbers fascinating?
* like science?
* easily do math in your head?
* like solving mysteries?
* enjoy counting things?
* like estimating, or guessing the amounts of things (like the number of pennies in a jar)?
* remember numbers and statistics easily (baseball statistics, sports scores, the heights of the tallest buildings in the world)?
* enjoy games that use strategy like chess and checkers?
* notice the links between actions and their results (otherwise known as cause and effect)?
* spend time doing brainteasers or logic puzzles?
* enjoy discovering how computers work?
* love to organize information on charts and graphs?
* use computers for more than playing games?

If you answered yes to any of the questions above, then you just identified some of the ways you're Logic Smart!

What Does It Mean to Be Logic Smart?

When you're Logic Smart, you may understand numbers and math concepts easily, enjoy finding patterns, and easily see how cause and effect works in science. You may enjoy figuring out riddles and brainteasers, or playing games that use strategy. You might be very interested in how computers work and even in writing programs for them. You could also show this kind of intelligence by solving math problems in your head, creating your own secret codes, doing science experiments, learning and programming with computer languages, or solving mystery stories.

Maybe you enjoy many of the activities above, or just a few of them. Either way, there's something that ties all of these activities together—and that's *logic*. Think of logic as a tool that helps you solve problems. When you apply logic to a problem, you might break down the problem into smaller steps that you can complete bit by bit. You're also putting together patterns and creating rules when you use logic to solve a problem or answer a question. Logic can help you do math, crack a code, solve a brainteaser, or answer a science question.

When you're being Logic Smart, you do things like:

* Get curious and observe people, places, or things.
* Notice cause and effect (or how an action leads to a *re*action), and then put together relationships (why a *specific* cause leads to a *specific* effect).
* Ask questions about things you observe or want to know.
* Notice patterns in everything from numbers to nature to human behavior.

So, are you starting to see the logic in Logic Smart?

Logic Smart skills can help you do many different things—from math, to science, to computers. But any kind of problem solving counts when it comes to being Logic Smart. You can use logic when doing a word scramble, trying to solve a "who-dunnit," or simply organizing your art supplies.

Want a quick way to test your own Logic Smart skills? Try this brain-teaser: *Freida had nine pieces of candy, but she's eaten seven of them. All of her friends started out with nine pieces of candy each, too. Some of them have eaten six pieces, while others have eaten only four pieces. Freida and her friends only have 25 pieces of candy left among them. How many friends does Frieda have? Hint: There may be more than one answer.* (See the answer at the bottom of this page.) Before answering, notice how you go about solving the problem. Do you read the problem aloud and talk out the steps to solving it? Do you automatically grab a pencil and paper and start jotting down your ideas? Do you look to another person for help? Does something else go on in your mind? These are all keys to understanding how you use your Logic Smart abilities.

Well, did you get a right answer to the brainteaser? If you did, great! If you didn't, still great! Because simply trying to solve the problem made you stretch your logic muscles and sharpen those Logic Smart skills.

Even if brainteasers give you a brain ache, you may be very logical and can still have fun with logic. Think about the games you've played. They can be as simple as tic-tac-toe or as complicated as chess. Most games by their very nature involve logic. While playing, you need to create strategies and follow them logically to win. Maybe you never thought of yourself as Logic Smart, but you're a really good game player. If so, you're probably a lot more logical than you give yourself credit for.

What can being Logic Smart do for you?

* You can improve your math, science, and computer skills.

* You can figure out and understand how the world around you works.

* You can use it to help solve problems in many areas of your life.

Answer: There are two correct answers. Freida had two pieces of candy leftover. That means there were 23 pieces left among her friends. So Freida could have seven friends—one friend has five pieces left and the other six friends have three pieces each (for a total of 23 pieces). Or, Freida could have five friends—one with three pieces of candy left and four friends with five pieces of candy left (again for a total of 23 pieces).

Things you may do every day that use this intelligence:

solve brainteasers or riddles ▪ count things ▪ play games like checkers, chess, or Battleship ▪ read mysteries ▪ create your own codes or break codes that other people have created ▪ spend money and count out your coins and dollars ▪ tell time ▪ estimate things like how much time you spend on the school bus during the whole school year (days? weeks?) ▪ collect sports scores or stats like your favorite baseball player's batting average ▪ budget an allowance ▪ play games on the computer ▪ do homework or other activities on the computer ▪ organize your belongings by their patterns or shapes or sizes ▪ play with or use a calculator ▪ spend time in the kitchen: measure spices, estimate how long it takes to bake something, or figure out how to pull a meal together so all the foods are ready at the same time ▪ think about inventions that would make life easier or better ▪ study a globe, maps, or an astronomy chart of the stars and planets

MEASURING YOUR MATH KNOW-HOW

One of the most common ways you use your Logic Smart skills is through math. You might be surprised at the different ways you use math throughout the day—and not just in math class. Numbers are everywhere! You see numbers on your wristwatch, on the signs along the road, and on the money you spend. Think about how many times a day you count things: everything from the number of pancakes you ate for breakfast to how many minutes are left until school ends.

When you first start learning math in school, you discover some basic things about numbers and the rules for how they work, such as "greater than" and "less than." You learn that a gallon is greater than a quart. You find out that a centimeter is less than an inch. You're taught that three feet is equal to a yard.

Then you learn *calculations* (adding, subtracting, multiplying, and dividing). Calculations are the building blocks of basic math. Without an understanding of calculations, you would have a hard time moving on to more complicated math like fractions and percents. As you get older and take more advanced math classes, you'll rely even more on logic. You'll discover the amazing ways that numbers work together and you'll be able to solve problems like: *3x = 24; what does x equal?* (Pre-Algebra or Algebra is where you'll see math like this.) The steps may get more complicated, but luckily they'll stay pretty logical. After all, logic is really what math is all about.

You may be happy to know that there's more than one way to be good at math—a number of ways. For example, you might be very math intuitive, which might mean that you understand how to solve new kinds of math problems without anyone showing you how to do them. Or it might mean that you get the answer to a problem without having to go through the steps. If so, you may find it frustrating to have to slow down and do each step to show your teacher your work. Maybe when you're forced to stop and do each step, you make mistakes with your calculations. So your answer is wrong, even though the steps you used to solve the problem were right. It can be really frustrating when this happens on homework or tests!

Did You Know?

There are people called math savants who have super-calculator minds and can do amazing math problems in their heads in seconds. They can tell you what day of the week your birthday will fall on in the year 3057, or what 24,637,646 x 46,593,299 equals in the time it would take you to turn on your calculator!

The good news is you may be able to use a calculator to help you check your results and pinpoint where you made your error. (Still, it doesn't hurt to practice your calculations so you won't make too many mistakes, whether or not you have a calculator around.) Whenever you find an error you've made, file it away in your mind for the next time you solve this kind of problem—and ask yourself how you made the mistake (a missed step or a math error?)—so that you learn from your mistakes.

On the other hand, maybe you're one of those people who loves doing calculations. Do you enjoy counting, playing with numbers, and doing every step in a math problem no matter how small? Do you do these tasks quickly and accurately? Maybe you're not exactly intuitive about math but you like the processes involved in solving math problems. Or perhaps you're both intuitive *and* good at calculations. (Lucky you!)

No matter what your math style may be, you can have fun using these skills in and out of math class.

Some "number lovers" like to play with math in a really concrete way, meaning they like to see math in action. For example, maybe during a grocery shopping trip with the family they have fun comparing food prices, using coupons to save money, and predicting how much the total cost will be before the cashier rings it up. If you want to use math in a concrete way, you can do this in your own kitchen. Bake a batch of your favorite cookies but *double* the recipe. You'll be using measurements, calculations, and maybe even fractions. Now that's putting math to a practical—and tasty—use!

All of these activities can help you with another important part of math (and Logic Smart): understanding what the numbers actually *mean*. Numbers are used to explain a lot of things from how much it costs to get a new basketball to how far away the planet Mars is. Some of this information may interest you now and some of it may not be important to you until you are older. Either way, it could help you a lot in life to understand what numbers mean and look like in the everyday world. A lot of math is about money and measurements—how much something costs, how far away something is, how much of something there is. Learning how these measurements look and work in your daily life is a good way to make numbers have meaning for you.

Think about your family's grocery bill again. Is the bill about the same amount every time? If the grocery bill is pretty consistent, try the following experiment. (If your family's grocery bill isn't consistent, ask a parent about doing this experiment with the phone or electric bill.) Figure out about how many times your family goes grocery shopping every year. (Or how many times a bill is paid in a year.) Then figure out how much money your family spends in a year on groceries (or on the phone or electricity). Are you surprised at the amount? What else could that same amount of money buy? New bicycles for everyone in the family? A used car? Some rare comic books?

That exercise probably gave you a better idea about money and how much it buys (and sometimes doesn't buy). Try the following exercises to get a better feel for distances and measurements. To understand distances, it might help to get your teacher and your class involved. Your teacher and class can pick a place that everyone wants to visit, for example, the Grand Canyon. Find out how many miles away it is from your school. Then you and your class can "walk" to the Grand Canyon. Find out how many laps around your playground equal a mile. Then make a chart and have everyone keep a tally of how many miles they walk, jog, or run at school. When your class has logged the same number of miles as it takes to get to the Grand Canyon, you've "reached your destination." Maybe you can celebrate by posting pictures of the Grand Canyon around your classroom. If you and your class do this exercise, you'll probably be a lot more fit and have a much better idea of how far away places really are.

To understand what liquid amounts really look like, all you need is a bathroom, an empty gallon container (old milk jugs work well), water, and some time. Fill up your bathtub one gallon at a time with the gallon container (instead of running water straight into the tub from the tap). How many gallons did it take? Did it take more water than you thought it would to fill up the tub? How much water do you think your family might use taking baths in a week? A year?

Did You Know?

Here's an important number: You have a 1 in 383 chance as a working adult of becoming a millionaire in any given year when you grow up. (Better odds than winning the lottery.)

What do these exercises add up to? A lesson in estimation. *Estimating* means that you do rough calculations on how much of something there is (or that you need) without actually counting it out. Basically you make your best guess—but you guess by trying to take different pieces of information into account. You make what's called an *educated guess.*

Some people are really good at estimating. They may never get exactly the right answer, but they're good at "being in the ballpark." You've seen contests where you've had to guess the number of marbles, pennies, or pieces of candy in a large jar. If you're good at estimating, you probably love those kinds of contests—and may often win them! Estimation can come in handy in your daily life when you've got to estimate how much paper you'll need for school, how many minutes you can spend on a specific question on your math test, or how many bags of leaves you have to rake up from the yard.

Have some fun and try your hand at estimating. Here are a few problems to flex your estimation mind with. Estimate:

* how many pencils you've used in school this year

* how many times you've written your name in your life

* how many footsteps you will need to go from the parking lot of your school to the front door of your classroom

* how many kids are in your school

These answers will be different for everyone. Remember: The key to estimating is making a good guess based on the information you have, not getting an exact answer.

There are a lot of fun (and practical) ways you can play with numbers and get better at math by exercising some logic. Math can be an entertaining way to explore logic and learn a little more about the world you live in. And if you win the occasional how-many-gumballs-in-a-jar contest along the way, then you've doubled the fun!

STUDYING YOUR SCIENCE SAVVY

Math is about problem solving, and so is science. There are other similarities, too. Both science and math involve (1) an eye for detail, (2) seeing patterns, and (3) the ability to make connections.

Science, in its most basic form, is about observing the world around you and creating theories about it. That can mean studying something as small as bugs in the yard or as vast as the stars. Whether you view something through the lens of a microscope or the eye of a telescope, you're gathering information, or *data.* The more you watch and notice, the more data you'll have.

Scientists create *hypotheses,* or unproven theories, to explain what they see. In order to test their hypotheses, scientists look for ways to gather more data to help them develop the theories further. This data is used to prove and disprove their theories. Sometimes the data supports part of the theory but not all of it. Every piece of information helps a scientist make a theory more detailed and eventually

> ## Did You Know?
> Science comes from the Latin word *scientia,* which means knowledge.

more accurate. Scientists often set up experiments to test their hypotheses and gather more data. This whole process is called the *scientific method,* and it can be used over and over again as a scientist creates new or revised theories and before a final answer is found.

Formal science consists of particular fields of study like physics, chemistry, and biology. Even if you aren't studying any of these subjects, you can use the basics of *scientific investigation* anytime in your everyday life. What is scientific investigation? Logic and problem-solving. Scientific investigation is using the scientific method to look for answers to your questions. It relies on logic just like math—both are about solving problems and answering questions. As you read earlier, the scientific method is a series of questions about how the world works and then the logical steps that scientists use to create theories and eventually answers for those questions.

Here's an example of how you might use the scientific method. You're walking down a path in the woods or in a park, and you see a hole. What made that hole? You make some guesses—a snake, a gopher, a woodchuck, a mouse, a lion. (Okay, maybe not a lion!) So you take a close look at the hole and decide that it looks too small for a gopher or a woodchuck to get into. So you reject those hypotheses. But what about the snake or the mouse? You watch the hole for a while to see if anything comes out of it or goes into it. After a bit, you see a mouse sticking its little nose out of the hole. That makes it seem pretty unlikely that a snake uses the hole for a home. And then, a little later, three mice go scurrying down into the hole. That's more evidence suggesting that it's a mouse hole. Of course, there still could be a snake or something else down there (possibly trying to eat the mice!), but you've

Did You Know?

These are all types of science:

Oceanography (the study of the ocean and all of its systems), Biology (the study of living things), Zoology (the study of animals), Entomology (the study of bugs), Marine Biology (the study of animals and things that live in the water), Geology (the study of rocks and the earth), Vulcanology (the study of volcanoes), Botany (the study of plants), Astronomy (the study of the stars, planets, and objects in the sky), Optics (the study of light and how it behaves) just gathered some good data that supports the hypothesis that this is a hole made by a mouse. (Or at least it supports that it's a hole where some mice live. Some other creature might have actually made the hole—that's another question to ask!)

Maybe you use this kind of organized and logical thinking all the time in your daily life. If so, you might be a future scientist. Science may be your favorite class in school, and you may love designing projects for local science fairs. Maybe you've got a chemistry set at home and you like doing experiments. Maybe you have other scientific tools like a magnifying glass, a microscope, or a telescope.

Perhaps you're a born observer, someone who's always asking questions about the world around you. *Why is the sky blue? Why are so many plants green? Where do rainbows come from?* Do you look for ways to answer your questions? Do you find out how other people have answered them?

Or perhaps you enjoy following what's going on with science in the news: finding out about new theories about why the dinosaurs died out, or how scientists think the universe was created, or the discovery of new animals and plants in the deepest parts of the ocean. Or maybe you're excited about the actual use of science in technology—space exploration, doctors using lasers in surgery, or artificial intelligence in computers. Wanting to know how things work and how other people—and scientists—use their Logic Smart abilities is another way that you are using your own Logic Smart abilities. Maybe you get ideas and information from these people that you use in your own life, or maybe you just feel better knowing answers to some big questions.

It seems as if new discoveries are coming out every day and faster than ever before. And yet, there are still a lot of questions to answer and scientific

Did You Know?

The sky is blue because of sunlight. Sunlight is made up of a lot of different colors of light mixed together even though sunlight usually just looks white. Some colors of light move through air, dust, and gases (the earth's atmosphere) better than others. Blue light tends to get shoved around a lot by air and dust. So, the blue sky you see when you look up is blue light that has been shoved out of the "white" sunlight by all of the air in our atmosphere.

mysteries left to solve. For every new discovery, several new questions are raised—which means that scientists will always have something new to keep them busy!

COMPUTING YOUR COMPUTER SKILLS

Logic is also important for computers. The languages that are used to run the many different software programs in computers are logical languages. One simple programming language that you might have learned in school is called Logo. Logo is an interesting programming language because it's designed to teach you the process of learning and thinking. Logo can be used for very basic tasks or for very complicated ones. It can be used in many different ways from math and music to science and robotics.

Often when you're first learning Logo, you'll use it to move around a small picture on your computer screen. In order to make the picture—for example a picture of a turtle—move, you have to figure out where you want it to go and what it will take to get there. You have to break down the movement into small pieces or steps. Then you have to write instructions for each step teaching your turtle where to go. So to get your turtle to walk in a square, you'll need to figure out how long each side of the square is and where the turtle needs to turn to start a new side of the square. If you and the turtle get bored with walking in a square (it can happen), you may decide to have the turtle walk in different, more complex shapes, which use more steps and more complicated instructions.

You use logic (and Logic Smart) when you break down the turtle's walk into different pieces and write instructions for each one. This is the same logic you use when you work with any computer language. The language and the goals you're trying to achieve just may be more complicated. The same functions of logic hold true whether you are creating a Web page (or a Web site) or using a computer program to

> ## Did You Know?
>
> Some people who have great difficulty learning word languages (like English, French, Spanish, German) can easily learn certain computer languages. That's partly because different areas of the brain are used for word and computer languages, and a person may have difficulty using the word part of his or her brain but not the logical part.

build a database. You figure out what result you want or what problem you have to solve, break it into steps, and then "solve" each one by writing instructions for the computer.

Computers and logic can be a lot of fun together. Do you play games on your computer? If you do, you are using your Logic Smart abilities to figure out how the game works and to think up strategies that will help you win it. Behind the scenes of those games are a whole bunch of people using those same Logic Smart skills to create these games. The games are designed, programmed, and tested by people using Logic Smart, proving once again that you can have a lot of fun being logical.

Fun Ways to Become More Logic Smart

Here are some ways that you can expand and enjoy your Logic Smart skills. Try *any* activity that appeals to you no matter how Logic Smart you think you are.

1 **Play games that use strategy and logic.** Games like chess, checkers, or dominoes all rely on creating strategies and understanding your opponent's moves.

2 **Watch television programs that teach science and math.** Shows like *Nova, National Geographic, Zoboomafoo, ZOOM,* and *Cyberchase* on PBS and *Bill Nye the Science Guy* on Nickelodeon highlight important science concepts and innovations.

3 **Practice calculating simple math problems in your head.** Don't use a calculator or paper and pencil (though you can later if you want to check your answers). If you find you can do it with easier problems, practice with harder problems.

4 **Explore science.** Visit a science museum, planetarium, children's museum, exploratorium, or other institution where you can explore science and math ideas through a number of stimulating interactive exhibits. If a topic really interests you, visit a setting where you can learn more about it and see math and science concepts being used in daily life.

5 **Read magazines or newspapers that cover math and science news.** Examples include *National Geographic Kids, Odyssey: Adventures in Science, Contact Kids, OWL: The Discovery Magazine for Kids,* and more.

6 **Practice estimating things.** For example, estimate the number of raisins in a bowl, pebbles in a pile, marbles in a jar, or toothpicks in a box, and then check your answers by actually counting them out one by one. Put on an estimation contest at school or in your neighborhood!

7 **Do brainteasers.** Get a book of brainteasers (or find a Web site that includes lots of fun math games and brainteasers) and solve them by yourself or with your friends or classmates.

8 **Have a special "math day" or "science evening" with your family.** Play math games, do science experiments, solve brainteasers, or learn together about science discoveries in the news.

9 **Write down ten questions about how the world works that you'd like answered.** (For example, "Where do rainbows come from?") Find the answers by looking in the encyclopedia, using the Internet, asking your parents or teachers, or doing experiments that you create yourself.

10 **Join a math or science club at school.** If your school doesn't have one, talk to a teacher about helping you start your own. Or maybe you'd like to start a less formal group with your friends or family and focus on something specific like stargazing.

11 **Find a book or Web site on science experiments you can do with things you have around your home.** Make sure you do experiments (or create your own) under proper supervision. This might lead you to create a science project that you can enter into a science fair at your school or in your community.

12 Get a tutor or find a classmate to help you with science or math if these subjects are hard for you. Someone who understands and loves math and science can make these subjects come alive for you!

13 Teach someone else math and science ideas that you've learned. You'll find that the more you have to explain an idea, the better you'll understand it yourself. Then find someone (a parent, friend, sibling, or teacher) who'll teach *you* more advanced math or science that you're curious about.

14 Pay attention to the use of numbers in the news. What do they really mean? If a new space probe has traveled 43 million miles to reach Mars, try to understand how far that actually is in a way that you can actually grasp; for example, how many round trips across the United States would it take to equal those 43 million miles to Mars?

15 Find out about the origins of math in different cultures. The ancient Maya and Arab cultures contributed a lot to the development of math ideas that we still use today, and they even had their own "calculators." Learn to use an abacus or other type of calculating device developed by another culture.

16 Build your own Web page or site. If you'd like, learn a computer language like HTML or Java to help you do it. (See the resources on page 63 for a Web site for kids that teaches you how to do this.)

17 Notice how you solve problems. As you solve problems in math or science class at school, observe what goes on in your mind, and notice what particular things you do with your mind that either help you or slow you up in the process.

What If You Think You Lack Logic Smarts?

Maybe you feel like Logic Smart doesn't make much sense to you. Hopefully in this chapter you've seen ways you already use your Logic Smart skills. Remember you don't have to be a math or science genius to be

Logic Smart. You might show your Logic Smart with a real knack for organizing objects or events, or through a love of drawing intricate geometric shapes.

Logic Smart gets used in all kinds of activities and a lot of them are in the smarts that you may feel most comfortable in. And that's handy. You can always use the smarts you're strongest or most comfortable in to become more Logic Smart.

Here are seven ways to do it:

 If you're Word Smart: Write and solve your own word problems. Talk through math problems (either by yourself or with others). Look for patterns in words and language. Read books with math themes like *The Phantom Tollbooth* by Norton Juster, *Math Curse* by Jon Scieszka, or *A Gebra Named Al* by Wendy Isdell.

 If you're Music Smart: Create your own raps or songs to learn your math facts. The times tables have a strong natural rhythm and can be sung to the music of your choice. Try solving problems or learning math facts to a beat.

 If you're Picture Smart: Visualize or draw out quick pictures or sketches of the logic problems you're working on to help you see different ways to solve them.

 If you're Body Smart: Use objects you touch and move around like dice, cards, beans or counters, and puzzle shapes to help you solve problems. Practice math facts while jump-roping, jogging, or walking.

 If you're People Smart: Play card games with friends or family. Start a math review group. Ask others for math help when you need it, and help others who ask you when you can.

 If you're Self Smart: Get fun books of puzzles and brainteasers that will help you work on math or logical thinking, and work to solve them on your own. Use your own quiet time to practice facts or think through math or science concepts.

If you're Nature Smart: Think about real-world applications of math. If you're working on fractions, what's something in your life you might need to divide into equal parts? Pizza with friends or ingredients when you're cooking? Can you think of other examples? Look at patterns and math in the environment. Nature is filled with examples of math: Check out pinecones, pineapples, or beehives. They have patterns that are "famous" for their regularity.

What If You're a Logic Leader?

If you love Logic Smart, you can always find new and interesting ways to explore it. The wonderful thing about logic is that it builds on itself. If you enjoy math, start learning more complicated math concepts. If science holds your attention, design science experiments and enter them in science fairs; see if you can actually meet and talk with real scientists about what they study and do. And computers can be used to explore both science and math further. Or you can focus on computers for their own sake. If you made a Web page, try building a site that's more complex. Learn computer languages that are more complex than Logo. (You might check out Java or C++.)

Your Logic Smart skills can also help you build your other intelligences. Here are some Logic Smart ideas you can use to help you understand and develop the other intelligences in school and in life.

 For Word Smart, read mysteries. The same logic and deductive reasoning that you use in math and science can help solve the "who-dunnits" that you read. Read science magazines or write about your favorite science topics.

 For Music Smart, listen for patterns in music. Complicated percussion music (with lots of different beats and rhythms) might appeal to you, with all of its many patterns working together.

 For Picture Smart, try creating visuals for math and science, like graphing science experiment results. Look for visual patterns, and even beauty, in science. For example, look at fractals, crystals, or prisms that divide out the light spectrum, and the shapes of snowflakes and *diatoms* (tiny organisms that live in water) under a microscope. Write a short computer program that creates colorful shapes or experiment with a computer animation program.

 For Body Smart, try playing sports that rely heavily on strategy. It will make it more interesting for you and you might become a great player even if your physical skills are less developed. Follow scores and stats on different sports and figure out how they tie in to an athlete's or a team's performance.

 For People Smart, play games with other people that emphasize strategy and logic. Chess, checkers, card games, and most board games are all good options, but there are many others to choose from. Notice how other people play the game and figure out why they make the moves they make to help you improve your own game.

 For Self Smart, look for patterns in your own life. Does understanding more about the world through science make you think about your place in it? Create a Web page for yourself or for a cause that you believe in.

 For Nature Smart, explore the life and earth sciences like biology or geology to learn more about nature and how it works. Ask questions about nature: *Why do leaves change colors in the fall? How do birds know where to migrate?* Look for answers.

Look to the Future

What can you do with your Logic Smart skills when you get older? A lot of very different things. Some of the careers you might look into include:

accountant ▪ air traffic controller ▪ appraiser ▪ astronaut ▪ auditor ▪ banker ▪ bookkeeper ▪ budget analyst ▪ climatologist ▪ code-breaker/cryptoanalyst ▪ computer programmer ▪ data analyst ▪ economist ▪ electrician ▪ engineer (mechanical, civil, electrical, chemical) ▪ epidemiologist ▪ financial aid officer ▪ foreign exchange trader ▪ forensic scientist ▪ information scientist ▪ insurance actuary ▪ insurance agent ▪ investment analyst/researcher ▪ loan officer ▪ mathematician ▪ meteorologist ▪ mortgage broker ▪ physician ▪ pollster ▪ population ecology analyst ▪ purchasing agent ▪ science teacher ▪ scientist (biologist, chemist, physicist, astronomer, geologist, botanist, oceanographer) ▪ statistician ▪ stockbroker ▪ technical writer ▪ technician ▪ treasurer ▪ video game designer/programmer ▪ Web master/programmer ▪ and many more!

Get Smart with These Resources

Books

1000 Playthinks: Puzzles, Paradoxes, Illusions & Games by Ivan Moscovich (New York: Workman Publishing, 2001). A large and colorful book chock-full of brainteasers and puzzling problems to solve. From beginner to ultra-challenging, the puzzles are broken into different categories from math to visual.

Challenge Math: For the Elementary and Middle School Student by Edward Zaccaro (Bellevue, IA: Hickory Grove Press, 2000). If you like math, this is the book for you. Move from challenging to Einstein-level problems in percentages, algebra, ratio and proportions, statistics, and more, with clear explanations, fun facts, and silly cartoons.

Explorabook by John Cassidy (Palo Alto, CA: Klutz, 1992). A fun, highly interactive book that explains a wide range of science subjects including optical illusions, magnetism, light waves, and biology through lots of experiments. A mirror, a diffraction grating, and an agar growth medium (among other items) are included in the book to use in the experiments.

The Great Book of Mind Teasers and Mind Puzzles by George J. Summers (New York: Sterling, 1986). A book of classic puzzles designed to sharpen your logic skills as well as provide hours of entertainment.

Head to Toe Science: Over 40 Eye-Popping, Spine-Tingling, Heart-Pounding Activities That Teach Kids About the Human Body by Jim Wiese (New York: John Wiley & Sons, 2000). Want to find out how much air your lungs hold? Or how to figure out how tall a person is from the size of her feet? Arranged by body systems, the projects in this book will answer these questions and more using things found around your house and explaining the science involved. Lots of fun sidebars and useful illustrations.

Math Curse by Jon Scieszka (New York: Viking Children's Books, 1995). The character in this book wakes up one morning to find that the entire world has turned into a problem, a math problem that is. Each event in her day creates a new set of math problems for her to solve to overcome her math curse.

Real World Algebra: Understanding the Power of Mathematics by Edward Zaccaro (Bellevue, IA: Hickory Grove Press, 2001). Translate the real world into algebra and make numbers work for you in the real world. Algebra and money, levers, percents, proportions, and more are covered. Filled with facts, cartoons, and problems to solve.

Organizations

The Exploratorium
3601 Lyon Street
San Francisco, CA 94123
(415) 397-5673
www.exploratorium.edu
This famous science museum in San Francisco is noted for its interactive hands-on exhibits on science, art, and human perception. Explore math, take an expedition to Antarctica, and learn about the science of sports (just for starters) at the museum's Web site.

Other

ScienceKits.com, Inc.
785F Rockville Pike, Suite 515 • Rockville, MD 20852 • (301) 294-9729
www.sciencekits.com
Want to do your own experiments? From chemistry sets to growing crystals, these makers of science kits for kids can help you do all of this and more. You can do everything from testing for environmental pollution to assembling a model of the human skeleton to building a robot.

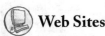 **Web Sites**

Chem4Kids
www.chem4kids.com
Easy-to-understand explanations of chemistry concepts. Learn about matter, the elements, atoms, and chemical reactions. Includes activities and downloadable flash cards.

Lissa Explains It All
www.lissaexplains.com
Lissa started this site when she was 11 years old to show other kids how easy it is to build their own Web pages and even Web sites. This site teaches you the basics and HTML, along with information on frames, tables, cascading style sheets, and more.

Mad Scientist Network
www.madsci.org
Ask real scientists questions (sponsored by Washington University Medical School in St. Louis, MO). If you have questions about how to make a food battery, the earth's magnetic poles, how caffeine works in the human body, or what color is, this is the site for you. You'll find answers to all of these questions and many others.

Neuroscience for Kids Site
faculty.washington.edu/chudler/neurok.html
From brain basics to sensory systems, this site leads you through the human brain and nervous system. Filled with interesting facts (Are the brains of girls and boys different? Is laughing good for you?) and fun brain games and experiments.

Science Learning Network
www.sln.org
This site has lots of great science information. Read about current events in the field, the science of everyday things, and much more.

Chapter 4

Picture Smart

Quick Quiz

Do you:

* remember faces better than names?

* like to draw out your ideas or make sketches to help you figure out problems?

* think in pictures and easily see objects in your mind?

* enjoy building things?

* like taking things apart and putting them back together?

* work with art materials like paper, paint, and markers?

* enjoy watching movies or videos?

* play lots of video games?

* notice the styles of clothing, hairstyles, cars, bikes, or other everyday things?

* read or draw maps for fun?

* enjoy looking at photos and pictures and talking about them?

* see patterns in the world around you?

* draw or doodle a lot?

* draw things in great detail or realistically?
* remember in pictures or images things that you've learned?
* learn by watching people do things?
* do visual puzzles, mazes, and optical illusions?
* like building models or things in 3-D?

If you answered yes to any of these questions, then you just identified some of the ways you're Picture Smart!

What Does It Mean to Be Picture Smart?

Picture Smart is mainly about learning and thinking in pictures—but there's much more to it than that. You may have a good memory for faces or places, or you may notice little details that other people usually overlook. In general, you probably remember many of the things you've learned in the form of images instead of words. You might have a strong sense of how objects relate to each other in a given space *(spatial intelligence);* for example, you may be able to rearrange your room several times in your head without ever having to move any furniture. You could show this type of intelligence by reading maps and finding your way around unfamiliar places, or by being good at taking things apart and putting them back together again.

Take a look around you. What sort of colors, shapes, pictures, textures, objects, and other things do you see? Now close your eyes. What kinds of images appear in your mind? These two worlds—the world of the imagination and the outer world you see—and how you combine them are key to being Picture Smart. Picture Smart abilities allow you to take what you see with your own eyes or what you imagine in your "mind's eye" and transform it into something that other people can see or touch. That's why Picture Smart is the intelligence of the artist *and* the inventor. Some Picture Smart people show this intelligence through activities like art, photography, movie making, or design, while others express it through architecture, model-building, engineering, or inventing.

Do you ever doodle on the sides of your homework? Maybe you doodle while doing other things—listening to your teacher in class, watching television, or talking with a friend on the phone. When you doodle, you're not wasting time, you're being Picture Smart. There are experts who say that doodling may actually help some people think better, because it exercises certain areas of the brain (including the spatially smart parts). You're in good company when you doodle. Some very famous thinkers used doodling or drawing to help them think better, like Thomas Edison (inventor of the light bulb), who kept sketch diaries of his ideas. Charles Darwin, known for his theory of evolution, filled sketchbooks with pictures of trees (drawings that helped him think about how different species divided like the branches of a tree). You might want to keep your own doodle diary or sketchbook to draw ideas that come to you: you never know what inspiration they might lead to.

Some Picture Smart people have a hard time in school. That's because most schools spend a lot of time focusing on words and numbers, rather than on pictures. Because Picture Smart people tend to think in images instead of words, they may have trouble remembering facts or ideas that are expressed in words or numbers. Experts have found that many kids who are identified as "learning disabled" (LD) or dyslexic are actually quite Picture Smart. They may be excellent artists or cartoonists, or they may be great at fixing or building things—but it may be hard for them to find ways to show these strengths in school.

Things you may do every day that use this intelligence:

draw, paint, or use other art materials for fun ▪ make collages ▪ create sculptures out of clay, papier-mâché, or interesting objects ▪ play with blocks, wooden sticks, or anything else that you can use to build 3-D objects ▪ watch movies or videos ▪ sketch out pictures to help you think through ideas or solve problems ▪ draw comics ▪ make movies with a video camera and a computer ▪ make animated cartoons on the computer or draw them by hand ▪ build models ▪ invent things ▪ collect interesting objects and make an attractive display ▪ decorate your room or other areas of your home ▪ keep a scrapbook ▪ play with visual puzzles or optical illusions ▪ take pictures (photography)

If you're Picture Smart, find ways to use this intelligence to your advantage. For example, if you have to memorize the 50 U.S. states, study a map instead of a written list of state names. You can close your eyes and picture where the states are. Using your visual memory comes in handy, especially when you're studying.

What can being Picture Smart do for you?

* You can use it to create different kinds of art.

* You can use it to solve problems and brainstorm new ideas.

* You can use it to design and build things from models to buildings.

Here are some ideas for improving your Picture Smart abilities both in and out of school:

* Talk with your teacher about ways you can add visual interest to class reports and homework. Find out if you can chart or draw out what you've learned.

* Volunteer to make posters for your classroom. The posters can be decorative, or illustrate class interests or rules, or showcase topics that your class is currently studying.

* Ask for more arts and crafts activities in the classroom.

* Suggest field trips to art museums, galleries, an artist's studio, or an architect's office.

* Ask your teacher to present new ideas visually as part of teaching them. Slides, videos, charts, diagrams, and posters are all helpful. (You could even volunteer to help your teacher make or find them.)

* Suggest the class make a movie or cartoon using a computer with software that helps you edit.

* Design and build models to present information you've learned or as part of projects or reports.

> ### Did You Know?
> Even if you're blind, you can still be very Picture Smart. There are blind photographers, artists, and graphic designers. Photographer Otto Litzel put together a book on photographic composition after he'd become legally blind from a car accident.

BEING SMART ABOUT ART

You might have guessed that most artists are very Picture Smart people. Their visual minds and memories help them draw, paint, or do other forms of art with skill. Perhaps you enjoy making art yourself. Maybe you're into sketching or cartooning, doing watercolor paintings, creating crafts, taking photos, or sculpting with clay.

If you like creating art, it can be fun to see what other artists have done in the past and are doing now. Art museums are great ways to explore artists' creations. Many art museums have discount tickets for kids and days when visitors can get in for free. The museums may also have self-guided tours, so you can learn about what you're seeing as you explore at your own pace. You can also check out art galleries where the work of present-day artists is on display. If you don't have access to museums or galleries, you can visit many museums from around the world on the Internet. Your local library can be another great place to start. Illustrated art books are a wonderful way to learn and to spark your artistic imagination. As you view art or read about it, you can learn about techniques like color, light, and composition (how things are arranged in a drawing or painting).

Maybe you enjoy art but don't think you're very good at it. Try this experiment: Pick an object around you to draw—it can be anything from an animal to a box of cereal. Once you're done, take a critical look at it. Does it look like what you were trying to draw? Is it in proportion or are parts of it too big or too small? Did you add details and shading?

Sometimes when people have trouble drawing it's because they're trying to draw what they see in their head instead of what is right in front of them. In other words, they're sketching what their *mind* sees, not what their *eyes* see.

What's the difference? Suppose you're sketching a box of cereal. Instead of thinking about it as "a box of cereal," look at its rectangular shape, its lines and shadows, its shadings of dark and light. Begin again, this time drawing the lines and angles; then shade the darker areas to see what shapes they form. When you look at your drawing again, it may seem more like a cereal box. The more you practice, the more you can have fun experimenting with drawing things in many different ways. (If you're interested in learning more about how to draw, see the resources at the end of this chapter.)

> ## Did You Know?
> Vincent van Gogh painted over 800 paintings in his lifetime, but he sold very few of them (maybe only one!) while was alive. (He did trade his paintings for art supplies, though.) On May 15, 1990, his painting *Portrait of Doctor Gachet* sold in just three minutes for 82.5 *million* dollars—the most money ever paid for a painting!

Even if drawing isn't your thing, you might still be very Picture Smart and good at art. There are lots of other ways to create art and to express yourself visually. Here are some ideas you can try:

* **Sculpting in clay or papier-mâché.** This lets you explore shape, texture, and proportion in three dimensions.

* **Building mobiles.** Mobiles are hanging sculptures. They let you play with shape, space, and movement in three dimensions.

* **Photography.** This is an excellent way to look at how light and dark and color can be used in composition, or how they can be changed to affect the look of a picture.

* **Origami.** This folded-paper technique is a great way to have fun with shape and color.

* **Collage.** You make collages out of almost anything—different paper, cloth, photos, and even found objects. When you make collages you can play with color, shape, composition, and texture.

* **Computer graphics.** Computer graphics programs let you easily experiment with proportions, shapes, and how different visual pieces fit together by giving you the tools to create 3-D designs, complicated geometric forms, and even colorful animations.

These ideas are just the beginning. You might find that sculpting in clay leads you to an interest in *claymation,* making your own animated movies with clay characters instead of with drawings. (The movie *Chicken Run* is a great example of claymation.) Or you might find that making collages gets you interested in learning how to make stained glass. Your creative and artistic interests could lead you to keep creative scrapbooks,

> ### Did You Know?
> Leonardo da Vinci was incredibly Picture Smart. Not only is he thought of as a great artist and famous for painting the *Mona Lisa,* he also invented many things and left notebooks of sketches and ideas for inventions he never got around to building. He taught his art students to look for pictures and images in the cracks of plastered walls, in clouds, and in other random formations.

make stationery for friends and family, create your own comic books, or even decorate a room at home. You might also develop an interest in arts and crafts and choose to explore activities like pottery, sewing and designing clothes, weaving, needlework, jewelry making, or working with wood.

Many of these artistic activities take some physical (or Body Smart) ability. For example, they may require fine-motor skills such as dexterity and a good sense of touch, as well as hand-eye coordination. (Read more about these skills on pages 92–93 in Chapter 5.) Because you're still growing and changing, you may find that your hands don't always work as well as you want them to, which can be especially frustrating if you enjoy art. Are there times when you have a picture in your head of what you want to create or draw, but you aren't able to do it as

> ## Did You Know?
>
> Grandma Moses, a famous American folk art painter, started painting in her 70s—when her arthritis got too bad for needlework!

well as you want to yet? Well, the key word in that sentence is *yet*. As with learning how to play a musical instrument or a new sport, *time* and *practice* are what you need: these two things help you develop your physical skills.

BEING PICTURE SMART IN 3-D

You might be surprised to discover you can be very Picture Smart without being good at, or even interested in, art. One of the most important things about this intelligence is the ability to understand *space*—not space, as in the planets, but the space that surrounds you and the objects within it. Many Picture Smart people have the ability to think in three dimensions (3-D). To understand why this is important, it helps to know the difference between two dimensions (2-D) and three.

Something that is two-dimensional is flat, like a picture or a photograph. There's no depth or layers to it. But a 3-D object *does* have depth and layers. Think of it as the difference between seeing a picture of a bottle and being able to hold an actual bottle in your hand. Being able to touch and experience a bottle in 3-D means you can see the bottom and top of it, hold it up to the light, fill it with water, and even drink from it.

To give you another example, consider the difference between looking at a maze on paper (2-D) and actually walking through one. It's a whole different experience!

With spatial intelligence, you have the ability to imagine things in your head in three dimensions. Not everyone can do this, so if you can that's great! This means you see things in your mind as if you could actually hold them and touch them. You can probably move these objects around in your mind and look at them from different angles.

The world we live in and move around in is three-dimensional. So you can see why being able to think in 3-D is an important ability. It can help you do simple everyday things, like figuring out if all your schoolbooks will fit in your backpack, or more difficult things like determining whether you can make that goal in soccer from where you're standing on the field.

Here's an example of what it's like to think in three dimensions. Close your eyes and imagine an ice cube. Now, turn that ice cube around in your mind so you can see it from different angles. Maybe you can see it melting in your mind and getting smaller!

Make this "test" more complicated by imagining three golf balls in a row, colored green, blue, and red from left to right. Picture taking the red golf ball and putting it between the other two balls. Can you do that? If you can, then you're moving images around in mental space. By moving the golf balls around, you've demonstrated that you have a three-dimensional world in your mind and can move through it just like you can move through the world around you.

Of course, you may be able to create far more complicated 3-D pictures in your mind than ice cubes and golf balls. If you'd like to experiment, try imagining the following scenes in your mind:

* your favorite car

* a kickball game

* the inside of a washing machine

* an ice-cream cone

* where you live

* the bottom of a lake or an ocean

* a yellow rhino wearing a purple sweat suit while jumping rope

* your teacher walking on the ceiling of the classroom

Could you see those images? If you couldn't, that's all right—you may be Picture Smart and not be able to picture them clearly. And you may still have a very vivid imagination that comes to life when you create your own images and scenes. If you were able to picture those scenes, could you see them and move things around in 3-D? Try this exercise again sometime if you want to keep practicing and building your 3-D thinking skills.

What can you do with a 3-D mind? The short answer is: almost anything. You can use it to amuse yourself (by picturing your teacher walking on the ceiling), or you can use it to actually solve problems. For example, you could figure out the best way to organize your homework area; easily solve math problems about space, size, and measuring; or come up with plays for your school's basketball team.

There are creative ways to combine spatial intelligence with a love of art, too. For instance, how about design? Picture Smart people who become designers are responsible for the images you see around you every day. They design ads and articles in magazines and newspapers; they design and put together the books you read (like this one!). They make Web sites, video games, and computer games look more fun and interesting. They design cars and trucks. Next time you're in a store, pay attention to the designs you see in everything from board games to bedspreads. Notice the displays and the store windows, too. Picture Smart people had their hand in those designs, too.

Did You Know?

Industrial designers design everything from vacuums to computers to cars. Almost anywhere you look around your home or school you see their handiwork. They design the shape and look of a product. They also think about how people are going to use a product, so designers also consider how to make a product safe and easy to use.

Architecture, or designing buildings and structures, is another example of how 3-D thinking can lead to creativity and problem-solving, but on a bigger scale. In a way, architecture is the ultimate in three-dimensional thinking. Architects create structures (sometimes huge ones) in which people live, work, shop, and attend events, so they have to imagine in 3-D all the things that will take place in that building.

Every building begins as a 2-D drawing or sketch. This sketch is turned into a *blueprint,* or detailed plans, that explains how the different layers of the building have been designed. Architects usually build a model (often several of them) while they're designing a building. These models can become incredibly elaborate, but they can also be *mock-ups,* or rougher structures, that help the architect think through different design ideas and spot problems or flaws in the design.

Many architects, like Frank Lloyd Wright and Antonio Gaudí, are famous for their artistry as well as their overall building designs. Wright was noted for his creative, organic, and open architecture. If your home has a living room or an open floor plan, then you have Frank Lloyd Wright to thank for it. He completely changed the nature of living space in America and most homes have at least small elements of his designs in them. Wright also designed furniture and art glass to go into his buildings. Gaudí was a famous Spanish architect whose buildings usually made very strong artistic statements. Some of his buildings were covered in detailed decorations and sculptures like the Sagrada Familia Church in Barcelona, while others were so curving that they almost look warped or as though they're melting into the sidewalk! Many architects incorporate different kinds of art like sculpture and stained glass into their designs.

If you thought you had to be a lot older to come up with these kinds of ideas, consider Maya Lin, who was only 21 years old when she won a national contest to design a memorial in Washington, D.C., for Vietnam veterans. Today, her design for the Vietnam Veterans Memorial stands between the Washington Monument and the Lincoln Memorial. She also designed the Civil Rights Memorial in Alabama, using a speech from Dr. Martin Luther King Jr. as her inspiration. Both an architect and a sculptor, Maya thinks about what her work is supposed to represent emotionally as well as how it should fit into its environment. She finds inspiration for her Picture Smart designs from images all around her, from Japanese gardens to Native American structures. Just think what you might accomplish someday if you polish up your Picture Smart skills!

THE POWER OF INVENTION

Since being creative and thinking in 3-D can be used to solve problems, Picture Smart is also one of the intelligences of the inventor. Inventors, artists, and designers have the ability to realize their inner ideas in the world around them. Where artists see ideas for their art, inventors often see problems that need solutions. Some of these are everyday problems—how to clean more efficiently, how to travel faster and more safely, or how to store huge amounts of information (in other words, the invention of the vacuum cleaner, the car, the plane, seatbelts, and the computer).

Do you see problems that you'd like to solve? Have you invented things? If you're looking for ideas, think about things you may do everyday: chores, sports, homework, hobbies, school, shopping, and volunteer work. All of these activities have problems that are waiting to be solved by an invention. Kids just like you have invented everything from an adjustable broom to a driver's license scanner. They've even patented their inventions!

Like writers and artists, inventors often get their ideas from daydreams. Daydreams are the pictures that your mind comes up with while you're awake, without effort and usually while you're not thinking of anything important. Sometimes daydreaming can be a bother, especially if you're trying to concentrate on something else (like your homework or your teacher's words). But if you learn how to *use* your ability to daydream, it just might lead to some really great ideas. Scientists have discovered amazing things because of their daydreams.

> ## Did You Know?
> Nicola Tesla was a great daydreamer and inventor. He developed the Tesla Coil and the AC generator that helps run many of our machines, among hundreds of other inventions. It's said that he designed his inventions in his mind and that he could even "test" his machines in his mind. He'd turn on one of these machines, then go off and do other things for a few weeks, and finally come back and check his imaginary machine for signs of "wear"!

Albert Einstein was a great daydreamer and a good example of a "picture thinker." He was thrown out of high school in Germany, in part because he was always daydreaming about things that interested him! Einstein used to daydream about what it would be like to ride on a beam of light as it headed out into the edges of the universe. Using this image—and others like it—he came up with his theories of relativity, which are among the most important scientific ideas of the 20th century.

You can use your imagination (and your daydreams) to come up with brainstorms of your own. Here are a few problems that you can set your imagination to work on—think of them as possible inventions of the future:

* new methods of recycling

* creating fuel out of garbage

* new kinds of cars that don't pollute the air or crowd the highways

* living spaces that can be used on other planets

* a cheap method for taking salt out of sea water

* better ways to grow food and feed the hungry people of the world

* space ships that can travel to other galaxies in years instead of in lifetimes

* a way to stop the spread of nuclear waste and nuclear weapons

What other problems would you like to use your Picture Smart abilities for? As you envision these ideas, you might want to sketch them or try making your own movie about them. There's no end to the inventive things you can do with your Picture Smart mind.

Did You Know?

Some people have an *eidetic* imagination, which means they're able to see things in their mind's eye as clearly as you see the world around you right now. They're also able to interact with these images almost as if they were real objects. Have you ever had a very vivid nightmare or dream where everything felt so real, it almost felt like you were awake? That's a good example of what it's like to have an eidetic imagination. Eidetic images disappear for most people as they grow up (though some continue to develop their eidetic imaginations).

Fun Ways to Become More Picture Smart

Here are some ways that you can expand and enjoy your Picture Smart skills. Try *any* activity that appeals to you no matter how Picture Smart you think you are.

1 **Explore the world of art.** If there are museums where you live, make a point of visiting them and seeing the different kinds of art they have to offer. If you don't have access to art museums, go online. Many museums have virtual exhibits of their collections (or parts of them) at their Web sites. (A search engine like Google is a good place to start looking for museums online.) Reading books and magazines that are illustrated with great art or photography can also be a good place to start your explorations. Your librarian may have some suggestions for art books and magazines.

2 **Keep a visual journal.** Visual journals are great for sketching things you see during the day that interest you, ideas you have, or problems you're trying to solve. You can make this journal part of your writing journal, or it can be separate.

3 **Create a "picture library."** Collect images, pictures, and designs you like from magazines, newspapers, postcards, photographs you've taken, and any other source you can think of. You can keep them in a box or assemble them into a scrapbook or a collage for your wall.

4 **Take pictures of your day.** It can be fun to take pictures of the interesting things you see during the day. Or you could practice your photojournalism skills and record the events of your life over the course of several days or weeks. After the pictures are developed, pick out the best ones and put together an album or hang them on your wall. (You might even want to keep taking pictures of your life over the course of several months or years and look at how the pictures—and your life—change over time.)

5 **Create your own videos.** If you can get access to a video or digital recorder, you can do anything from making your own music video to creating a documentary to filming a movie where you write a script and get your friends to act in it. Many computers have easy programs that you can use to edit and add sound and credits to your masterpiece.

6 **Play games and work puzzles that pump up your Picture Smart abilities.** Pictionary is a classic visual game, and many games—3-D tic-tac-toe, checkers, and chess—rely on visual strategies and being able to "see" different moves before choosing the one you want to make. Jigsaw puzzles, Rubik's cube (or any 3-D puzzle), and mazes are all fun ways to work on your spatial abilities.

7 **Have fun with optical illusions.** Optical illusions are pictures that fool your brain or nudge it into seeing an image in more than one way. You can create your own optical illusions, too. (See the resources at the end of this chapter for more on how to do this.)

8 **Create on the computer.** There are many programs you can use to create on the computer. Programs like Adobe Photoshop alter photos and images. Programs like Adobe Illustrator let you draw on the computer screen, choosing different colors and textures with the click of a mouse. There are programs that can help you do anything from designing a car (computer-aided design or CAD programs) to creating your own cartoons.

9 **Take a class.** What are you interested in learning? How to draw or paint? The basics of architecture? How to take and develop your own photographs? Famous artists of the past? Different crafts? You can find classes on all of these topics and much more. Look for classes in after-school programs, in continuing education programs, at community centers, through museums (art and children's), at community colleges, online, and with private instructors.

10 **Create a "design studio" in your home.** Keep materials around to draw and build mock-up models of your inventions, ideas, or projects. You might want to include materials you can buy such as Legos, D-stix, hexaflexagons, and blocks, as well as household items that can be used for building like Styrofoam, glue, pipe cleaners, paper clips, soda straws, toothpicks, and clay.

11 **Create an "art smart" area in your house.** Good materials for you to keep around are pencils (with the softer pencil lead if you can find them), markers, colored pencils, modeling clay, construction paper, scissors, glue, glitter, tissue paper, paint, drawing paper, poster boards, foam-core board, and anything else that appeals to you. An easel or a corkboard to hold paintings and pictures while you work and a plastic tablecloth to protect floors and tables can be helpful, too.

12 **Spend a few minutes each day looking around you.** Enjoy small details like the angle of sunlight in your classroom in the afternoon, the different colors on a billboard, the shapes of the playground equipment, the lines of your favorite car, or anything else that captures your eye.

13 **Lobby for Picture Smart activities at your school.** Talk with your teacher or your principal about having more art in the classroom, developing a class unit on architecture, or organizing an inventor's fair for your school.

14 **Transform how you see the world.** Things like kaleidoscopes, telescopes, magnifying glasses, and microscopes all change how you see the visual world and let you explore what you see. Kaleidoscopes play with color, light, and patterns. (You can make your own kaleidoscope, see the resources section for how.) Microscopes and magnifying glasses make tiny things appear large and put into view a new world of patterns and shapes. Telescopes bring faraway things much closer—not only can you see the moon up close, you can see craters on its surface in detail!

15 **Look for interesting visual patterns in everyday life.** Patterns are all around you—from the "eyes" on the skin of a pineapple in the grocery store to rows of windows in a big office building. The more you look for visual patterns, the more you're likely to see them (for example, repeating squares in a row of houses or a pattern of crosses in a fence).

16 **Have a picture "conversation."** Have a conversation with a friend or family member by drawing pictures. Your partner draws something, you "answer" with a drawing of your own, and so on until you're finished "talking." After you finish your picture conversation, talk about it together and see if you were "talking" about what you thought you were with your pictures.

What If You Can't Picture Yourself as Picture Smart?

Maybe you find drawing stick figures challenging, have never been able to solve a Rubik's cube, or don't feel particularly inventive. Are you still Picture Smart? Absolutely! Just like every other intelligence, you use your Picture Smart abilities every day without realizing it. When you look at a bus or subway route map to find your stops, catch a baseball, or doodle on the side of your homework, you're being Picture Smart. If you can do those things, you can do a whole lot more!

And you can always use the smarts you're strongest or most comfortable in to become more Picture Smart.

Here are seven ways to do it:

 If you're Word Smart: Picture what you're reading or writing—a story can come to life when you picture what the characters are wearing or where they live. You can take this a step further by drawing pictures or maps, sculpting figures of the characters, or building models of the places you've read about in stories. If you love to write your own stories, look closely at the world around you for visual details that will make your words come alive for your readers. If you want to push your story-writing skills, try two versions of a story—write one using words and "write" the other using only illustrations. Which one do you prefer? Did the plot change when you drew your story?

 If you're Music Smart: Close your eyes when you listen to your favorite music and notice what images, colors, or shapes you see in your imagination or what kinds of daydreams you have. Sketch, paint, or model in clay what you see in your mind or how the music made you feel. If your daydreams had interesting ideas or objects in them, sketch or build a model of them. Music can be a great jumping-off point for all sorts of creativity and inventions.

 If you're Logic Smart: Maps and globes are great tools that mix Logic and Picture Smarts. When you play around with them you not only can work out distances and locations, you can also look for shapes and patterns. If you have a map of where you live, locate your home and your school and find as many different routes between them as you can. Another way you can work on your Picture Smart abilities is to draw your own puzzles or create mazes for other people to solve.

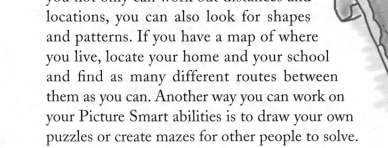

 If you're Body Smart: Use those wonderful hands of yours to solve jigsaw puzzles and other hands-on puzzles like a Rubik's cube. And don't forget to try your "hand" at different kinds of art: painting, sculpting, building, or drawing all get you moving in one way or another! You might find architecture especially interesting, since you can build 3-D models based on what you learn.

 If you're People Smart: Art can be a great way to get together with others. Creating a group mural, collage, or a movie will have you exploring different ways to be Picture Smart, while giving you the opportunity to meet new people or work with your friends. Face painting with your friends can be a fun way to get creative with your Picture Smart abilities (but make sure you have the proper paints and adult permission for this).

 If you're Self Smart: Art and images can be great ways to express complicated feelings. You can use the art you create to explore how you feel, or you can look for images from magazines and newspapers that capture and show your emotions. Create a collage of these images or place them in your journal as a way of expressing who you are and how you feel.

 If you're Nature Smart: Collect fallen leaves, feathers, seeds, pods, or other things from nature to create your own "natural art." Experiment further by making your own natural paints (many plants, flowers, and nuts contain natural colors and dyes) or painting with pine needles or feathers. If you live in a city, create a city collage or sculpture by collecting different items found naturally in that landscape. What items do you think you'll find? Bottle caps? Pigeon feathers? Advertising flyers? Cans and bottles?

What If You're a Picture Smart Pro?

Since there are so many different ways to be Picture Smart, you can have a lot of fun experimenting with them. If you're really art smart in 2-D, take your art into 3-D and use it to work on your spatial intelligence. If you're used to drawing, painting, or designing on the computer, experiment with modeling forms in clay and papier-mâché, building mobiles, and constructing models of your 2-D designs. If you love inventing, learn and practice the skills you need to design, build, and present your inventions to other people.

Your Picture Smart skills can help you build your other intelligences. Here are some Picture Smart ideas you can use to help you understand and develop the other intelligences in school and in life.

 For Word Smart, notice the visual images in what you read. How do they help the characters or setting come to life for you? How do the illustrations in a book help or detract from the story? Comics can be a great way for you to tell your own stories. As you write and draw your own comic book, notice how the pictures and words work together. Do you change the pictures to better tell the story? Does your original story idea change as a result of your illustrations? Read poetry, too, and notice the shape and flow of the words on the page. Often, poets are very concerned with the look of their poems as well as the words within them. Some poets write poems in the shape of something, for example an apple. Other poets, like Shel Silverstein *(Where the Sidewalk Ends)*, even illustrate their work.

 For Music Smart, listen to music while you make art, work on designs, or build inventions. Music can help the flow of creativity. You might find that your ideas become more detailed and your art improves as you listen to music. Try different kinds of music—you might like painting to pop, sculpting to reggae, building models to jazz, or designing your inventions to classical music. You might be surprised what works best for you. (A lot of artists use music for inspiration, see page 33 in Chapter 2 to find out more.)

 For Logic Smart, you might find that drawing your math problems or science experiments helps them make sense to you. So much of Logic Smart is about observation and seeing patterns—both of which you're really good at! So your ability to see visual patterns in the world around you can help you learn how to see patterns in new Logic Smart ways. Again, sketching out what you're thinking about or working on can help you see patterns and answers you might otherwise miss.

 For Body Smart, you may have noticed that a lot of the Picture Smart activities you do already involve using your body. Sculpting and building are both good examples. Artists of all kinds can be very physical in how they make their art. Painter Jackson Pollock, for example, put his canvases on the floor and walked all around them drizzling and splashing paint from different heights. Can you think of ways to become more physical in how you make your art? Learning more about your body and how it moves can help you be a better artist and designer or a more effective inventor as you think about how you move around and use objects.

For People Smart, use your design sense for causes you believe in. Your ability to paint and draw posters, design banners, or create a logo for a T-shirt could make you pretty popular if you volunteer your talents. By doing so, you'll meet and get to know people who care about the same things you do. Teaching can be another great way to reach out to others, whether you teach younger kids in a Head Start program or share a project with your Scout troop. Abilities you may take for granted like being able to draw, knowing how to use a camera, or having the skill to build elaborate 3-D models are often things that other people want to learn.

 For Self Smart, use your sketch journal for more than design ideas. Draw pictures about your day, what you see yourself doing in the future, or how you're feeling at the moment. There are many other ways to use your Picture Smart abilities to express yourself. Design your perfect bedroom, one that you feel really reflects who you are. Or design and sew a piece of clothing that makes a statement about you and how you feel about yourself.

 For Nature Smart, a strong spatial intelligence and an ability to read maps might make you a natural for orienteering. Orienteering is a sport in which you use a detailed map and a compass to find your way to specific places on the map. People usually do this sport in natural areas like the woods. If you prefer to be a little less goal-oriented, go to a nature spot like a park or a beach and take a good look around you. What are you most interested in? Plants? Animals? The shape of the land? Sketch or take pictures of the things that interest you most. If you'd prefer, draw a map of the area and sketch in as many features as possible.

Look to the Future

What can you do with your Picture Smart skills when you get older? A lot of very different things. Some of the careers you might look into include:

advertiser ▪ animator ▪ architect ▪ art teacher ▪ cartographer (a map maker) ▪ children's book illustrator ▪ cinematographer ▪ civil or mechanical engineer ▪ construction worker/ builder ▪ documentary maker ▪ drafter ▪ environmental designer (designs exhibits, signs, and store layouts) ▪ fashion/ clothing designer ▪ fine artist (includes: potter, jeweler, glass blower, painter, drawer, photographer, textile artist, sculptor) ▪ furniture designer ▪ geographer ▪ geometry or trigonometry teacher ▪ graphic artist ▪ graphic designer (includes: book/ magazine designer, packaging designer, sign and environmental designer, branding designer) ▪ interior designer (or decorator) ▪ inventor ▪ landscape designer ▪ medical illustrator ▪ movie maker/movie director ▪ movie special effects artist ▪ navigator ▪ packaging engineer (designs how to package products for sale or shipment—not the graphics that go on them) ▪ photographer ▪ photojournalist ▪ pilot ▪ product developer/industrial designer ▪ sailor ▪ surveyor ▪ urban planner ▪ Web designer ▪ window dresser ▪ and many more!

Get Smart with These Resources

Note: If you're invention minded, make sure you look at the resources in Chapters 3 and 5, too.

 Books

Absolutely Mad Inventions by A.E. Brown and H.A. Jeffcott Jr. (Mineola, NY: Dover, 1976). Learn about dozens of crazy inventions that have actually been patented like the edible tiepin.

A Book of Artrageous Projects by the editors of Klutz and The Metropolitan Museum of Art, New York (Palo Alto, CA: Klutz, 2000). Ever want to try painting (with paint you mixed)? Making stained glass? Embossing? Sun photography? You can do all of these things and more with this book, which comes with all the materials and attitude needed to unleash your creative self with more than 20 projects.

Castle by David Macaulay (Glenview, IL: Scott Foresman, 1982). This award-winning book tells the story of an imaginary castle in Wales built in the 13th century. The process, including the architecture, the engineering, the tools used, and what the workers did, is explained in detail and with intricate illustrations. One of a series that includes: *Pyramid, Cathedral, City,* and *Ship.*

Click: Fun with Photography by Susanna Price and Tim Stephens (New York: Sterling, 1997). An introduction to what can be done with a simple compact camera. Also comes in a kit with a 35mm camera and a photo album.

Complete Origami: An A–Z of Facts and Folds with Step-by-Step Instructions for Over 100 Projects by Eric Kenneway (New York: St. Martin's Press, 1987). Become your own origami factory with this book's clear directions, color diagrams, and fun projects.

How to Make Optical Illusion Tricks and Toys by Richard Churchill (New York: Sterling, 1990). Create more than 60 illusions, including tricks, drawings, and toys that you can put together.

The Kids' Book of Kaleidoscopes by Carolyn Bennete with Jack Romig (New York: Workman, 1994). Make art while learning about the science of light and color. Includes plastic safety mirrors, tube and turning end, plastic eyepiece and tube cover, color gels, and a collection of colored beads, gems, chips, and other materials to put in your kaleidoscope.

Looking at Pictures: An Introduction to Art for Young People by Joy Richardson (New York: Harry N. Abrams, 1997). From themes, techniques, and famous painters to how paint is mixed, canvases are stretched, and what goes on behind the scenes at a gallery, this book helps you learn how to appreciate art.

The New Drawing on the Right Side of the Brain by Betty Edwards (New York: Jeremy P. Tarcher/Putnam, 1999). A classic book on how to learn how to draw even if you never thought you could.

101 Amazing Optical Illusions: Fantastic Visual Tricks by Terry Jennings (New York: Sterling, 1998). This book contains a variety of colorfully illustrated illusions, plus brief directions for making some of them.

Take a Look Around: Photography Activities for Young People by Jim Varriale (Brookfield, CT: Millbrook Press, 1999). Full of great black and white pictures of the countryside taken by kids from the author's summer photography classes, this book also has descriptions of techniques, projects to try, and explanations of what makes each photograph in the book so good.

You Can Make a Collage: A Very Simple How-To Book by Eric Carle (Palo Alto, CA: Klutz, 1998). Use the easy instructions and the colorful tissue that comes with the book to learn how to create beautiful art collages from a master of the form.

 ## Other

Clay Animation Kit
Tech4Learning, Inc. • 10981 San Diego Mission Road, Suite 120 • San Diego, CA 92108 • 1-877-834-5453
www.tech4learning.com/products/claykit.html
This software helps kids create their own claymation movies. (It even includes the clay.)

 ## Web Sites

Children's Art Galleries, Juried Online Arts Festival
www.jolaf.com/resources/childrens_art.html
This online arts festival includes a list of art galleries online to which kids can contribute their art for display.

Invention Dimension
web.mit.edu/invent
An invention Web site and contest for older students sponsored by MIT. Includes a wonderful links section to explore many other invention sites for kids and an inventor of the week feature.

Chapter 5

Body Smart

Quick Quiz

Do you:

* like to move around and be active?
* learn physical skills easily and quickly?
* move while you think?
* enjoy acting in skits or plays?
* mimic or imitate people's gestures and expressions?
* play sports or do well in one particular sport?
* do crafts or build models with skill?
* dance gracefully?
* use movement to help you remember things?
* have good coordination or a good sense of timing?
* love recess?

If you answered yes to any of the questions above, then you just identified some of the ways you're Body Smart!

What Does It Mean to Be Body Smart?

Being Body Smart means you learn and think with your body. You also use your body to express yourself or your skills. You are probably comfortable in your body. You may be an athlete, or you may use your body artistically to dance or act. Or you may have more interest in using your hands to do activities like crafts, sculpture, building, mechanics, or fixing things. You could show this intelligence by being good at soccer, knitting or sewing with ease, creating sculptures out of clay, acting with flair in a drama, performing magic tricks, or being able to fix broken objects around your home.

People often don't think of their bodies as being "smart." You might assume that your body and your mind do very different things. After all, you do activities and actions with your body, and you think and learn with your mind. The body just seems to do its own thing—walking, climbing, bending, reaching, and so on. Right? Well, that's partially true. *But,* how is the body able to perform these actions? Through instructions from the brain.

You use many different parts of your brain in order to move—to run, dance, build models, play sports, tie knots, juggle, hike, and do any kind of physical activity. Each of these actions requires the quick and careful coordination of countless nerves, muscles, joints, and other body parts. If you had to tell each part of your body individually how to move, it would probably take you weeks to simply get out of bed in the morning! Your brain issues commands to your body quickly so that moving around and doing things takes seconds and not weeks. The fact that your body knows what to do when you want it to do it—and fast!—means your body is actually pretty brainy.

Did You Know?

The Romans (and the ancient Greeks) believed that you had to have a healthy body in order to have a healthy mind. They even had a saying for it: *Mens sana in corpore sano.* That's Latin for "a sound mind in a sound body." That's why they considered athletics to be so important.

What can being Body Smart do for you?

* You can become healthier by exercising and playing sports.

* You can learn to think and solve problems in a whole new way.

* You can use your body to express yourself artistically.

One of the many ways to be Body Smart is by expressing your skills physically. Physical skills take intelligence, too. A successful athlete has to be able to calculate speed, *trajectories* (angles and curves), and strategy, and have the coordination, endurance, and strength to pull it all together. That's a lot of brain work!

A baseball pitcher is a good example of someone who is Body Smart. A good pitcher has to have the strength to throw a 90-miles-per-hour fast ball. He has to plot the ball's trajectory (how it curves in the throw) and what kind of spin to put on the ball (how it moves or dips while airborne). And finally, he has to understand the best pitches to use to strike out as many players as possible. You might say a good athlete has to have a lot "on the ball"! It makes the whole idea of the "dumb jock" seem a little dumb, doesn't it?

It's not only athletics that demands physical skill. Consider the work of surgeons and dentists. These professionals rely heavily on their sense of touch, hand-eye coordination, and dexterity to do their jobs. So do carpenters, craftspeople, musicians, and mechanics. All of these people use their bodies in some way to understand and solve problems.

Being Body Smart is about *thinking* and *learning* through touch, movement, and motion as well as having physical skill. As you develop this intelligence, you can make better use of your senses, your hands, and your entire body—from the top of your head to the soles of your feet.

Things you may do every day that use this intelligence:

dance ▪ fix things ▪ build models ▪ arts and crafts (pottery, knitting, crochet, sewing, beading, weaving, painting, drawing, embroidery...) ▪ play a musical instrument ▪ play outside ▪ climb trees ▪ play games like marbles, jacks, or charades ▪ act in plays and skits ▪ do martial arts ▪ practice yoga ▪ play sports ▪ go for walks or hikes ▪ tie knots or do macramé ▪ play video games ▪ do imitations of other people or of animals ▪ do magic tricks ▪ practice handwriting or do calligraphy ▪ type on a keyboard (or use a calculator)

KEEPING IN TOUCH WITH YOUR BODY

When it comes to physical skills, you can be Body Smart with your whole body, or you can be Body Smart with very specific parts of your body, like your hands. That's why both athletes and surgeons are Body Smart. How do *you* show your Body Smart skills?

You might show your Body Smart best through competitive games—like soccer, volleyball, football, baseball, basketball, swimming, gymnastics, track and field, tennis, wrestling, or hockey. Or you might shine your brightest when you're competing against yourself through sports like skiing, snowboarding, inline skating, ice skating, skateboarding, or mountain biking. Perhaps you're not very competitive but you enjoy the *fun* of different kinds of sports and games and how they give your body a chance to run, move, stretch, and play.

To boost your body "smarts," try out as many different activities as you like, and find one (or several) you enjoy. No matter what sport or activity you do, and how skilled you think you are (or aren't), you're exercising your Body Smart skills. You're becoming more physically fit and improving important things like your:

* balance (how steady you are and how well you can stay upright)

* coordination (how well the different parts of your body work together)

* flexibility (being able to move your joints through their full range of motion)

* strength (how much power your muscles have to move against resistance)

* endurance (stamina, how long you can do an activity without getting really tired)

* reflexes (how quickly you respond to something physically)

By doing something that helps you feel good and be healthier, you're shaping up all of your other smarts, too!

Maybe your Body Smart skills are more finely focused. You might show your physical intelligence more through your:

* dexterity (how quickly, skillfully, and easily you use your hands)

* hand-eye coordination (how well your hands and eyes work together and share information)

* tactile sensitivity (how responsive your sense of touch is)

These skills often show an ability to work with your hands. You could use anything from wood to paper to a needle and thread.

In fact, the hands are one of the most intelligent parts of the human body. The smartest finger on your hand is actually your thumb. *Opposable thumbs,* which means that the thumbs can be placed against one or more of the other fingers on the same hand as the thumb, are what sets humans apart from most animals. (When you bring your index finger and your thumb together to form an "okay sign," you're showing off your opposable thumb.) Your thumb lets you pick things up, build, create tools, and develop new inventions. It takes a lot of body intelligence to be able to use your hands to work with tools. When you think about it, your opposable thumb (working with your other fingers, of course!) is the key to how human society was built and even how it runs now. Not bad work for the stubbiest finger of the lot.

People who work with their hands are using "fine" or "small motor" skills. These skills require good hand-eye coordination and dexterity—or the ability to do small movements with accuracy and speed. A lot of activities use these skills. Some are practical like typing, using a hammer or screwdriver to fix something, or sewing a button onto a shirt. Some activities are artistic like modeling with clay, making jewelry, or playing a violin or an oboe. Some activities are creative and fun like crafts, cooking, or magic tricks.

Hands are also used to literally feel out situations and solve problems. When you fix engines or anything mechanical like a watch or a toaster, you're using your hands to learn and understand the problem as you fix it. Surgeons and dentists also have to feel out problems and almost "see" with their hands when they're working on patients. From diagnosing problems to stitching up injuries, doctors, nurses, and veterinarians also use their sense of touch and dexterity in different ways to help them do their jobs.

> ## Did You Know?
> Some animals also make tools to do things, especially to get food. Scientists have seen chimpanzees (who also have opposable thumbs) and crows (who don't) make tools out of branches, rocks, sticks, and even wire.

THE MIND AND BODY CONNECTION

You may be wondering what being Body Smart has to do with being a smart thinker in other areas. Well, the answer is it has *everything* to do with the other intelligences! Your mind and body work together to gather and process information. In fact, they often do that better together than they could apart. The key to doing this successfully is learning to listen to your body when it's telling you something important. A good way to learn this is by doing activities that bridge the gap between the body and the mind, uniting them and using one to work with the other. Bringing your mind and body together can help you focus on and improve how you use your other smarts. Martial arts, tai chi, yoga, and meditation, which all take different approaches to working the mind through the body, are traditional bridging activities used in many cultures.

Martial arts include such disciplines as tae kwon do, karate, aikido, and judo. Most martial arts were developed several hundred years ago in Asia. The countries of China, Japan, and Korea are especially known for their different martial arts. Each of these cultures believed that the mind and body should work together as a unit. The different martial arts are examples of this belief in action. Traditionally, the mind must be very focused on the actions of the body and what those actions are supposed to achieve. Movement and strategy, ideally, flow together.

For example, when you practice a kick in tae kwon do, you don't just kick out casually while thinking about what you're going to eat for dinner. You focus all of your attention—your whole mind—on the kick. That way, your body and mind work together in harmony to make the kick really mean something. In many ways, the people who created the martial arts understood the idea of being Body Smart way before its time!

Tai chi was created hundreds of years ago in China. It is both a martial art and a series of exercises to promote a healthy body and a balanced spirit. Tai chi is a series of structured movements called forms. These forms are designed to improve balance, coordination, strength, and timing. While practicing the movements, you meditate, or focus your mind, on the movements. There are many different traditions of tai chi. What does all of this have to do with you? Tai chi is one way you can develop and learn about the body-mind connection.

Yoga is another physical tradition from Asia that works with the body-mind connection. It's very different from martial arts. Yoga was developed in ancient India and is practiced throughout the world today—even by a lot of famous actors, rock stars, and celebrities. Like tai chi, there are different styles or ways to do yoga. Usually when you do yoga, you put your body into different poses, which are often named after animals or things in nature (the downward facing dog, the cobra, the tree pose). You focus your mind, or meditate, on the different body positions as you do them. You also pay attention to your breathing, which helps you focus your mind and hold the poses.

But there's another way to look at the body-mind connection—and other ways to exercise it if martial arts or yoga don't interest you. Your body can work with your mind to help you solve problems and get creative ideas. In other words, you can actually *think* with your body.

Did You Know?

Millions of people in China begin their day by doing tai chi. Often you can see large groups of people in public parks doing tai chi together early in the mornings.

Consider Albert Einstein, a noted Logic Smart and Picture Smart thinker, who also *thought with his body.* Someone once asked him how he solved some of his hardest physics problems, and he answered that in part he used *muscular* processes. He got "gut feelings" about things. He not only used his body to help him think through his ideas and solve problems, but he even used his body to explain physics to other people! At one meeting, he explained his latest theory of the universe to a colleague by using his rib cage and his spine as a physical model to illustrate his ideas.

Gut feelings aren't just for Einstein—you have them, too. Gut feelings or physical responses can be your body's way of helping you think through information and feelings. If you come up with a really great idea for an invention or a skit, you might get goosebumps. A famous poet named A.E. Houseman talked about the hair on the back of his neck bristling up when he started writing something really good. If you're nervous about a test, a performance, or a big game, you might get "butterflies" in your stomach. These physical reactions are your body's way of telling you that you're on the right track, or that you need to pay attention to something important.

Did You Know?

Many famous artists and creative people do yoga to enhance their creativity and focus for their performances. Yo-Yo Ma, a famous cellist, does yoga during the intermissions of his longer concerts to help him relax and to maintain his energy and focus. The pop star Sting also does yoga before he performs a concert.

Your body can sometimes process information before your mind has had a chance to. Gut feelings, or instincts, can also help protect you and help you make better decisions for yourself. For example, you might be out on the playground at recess, and you start to feel nervous and tense. You don't see anything wrong yet, but your body has picked up on signals that two kids aren't getting along and may be getting ready to fight. So, what did your body pick up on? It could have been how the kids' movements and voices changed, or how people closer to them were starting to react and pull back from the tense scene.

Improving your body-mind connection is simply another way you can be the best at what's important to you. Whether that's collecting rocks, writing poetry, or beating an opposing team on the field, your body and mind can help each other process information in many different situations. No matter what your skills and interests are, listening to what your body is telling you and developing your instincts can help you grow and learn.

YOUR EXPRESSIVE, ARTISTIC BODY

The human body is a wonderful and versatile creation. Not only can you use your body to do things like play sports or type email, you also can use your body creatively and to express how you feel. Dancers, actors, mimes, and sculptors all use their bodies in artistic ways. Musicians and artists of all sorts use their Body Smart talents to create beauty.

Dancing is a form of creativity that uses your whole body. When you dance, you're not simply moving to music—you're communicating something to other people, or even to yourself. Some people use different dance forms to share feelings, tell stories, express ideas, or celebrate their culture or religious beliefs. Dance can be as simple as grooving to whatever song comes on the radio. Or dance can be complicated, fancy, and precise.

There are all sorts of ways to dance: swing, salsa, ballroom, ballet, hip-hop, jazz, tap, clogging, belly dancing, modern, folk, traditional. Some forms of dance like ballet are used for storytelling (the fairy-tale magic of *The Nutcracker Suite* is a good example of this). Other dance forms, particularly folk and traditional dances, started out as ways to express important ideas in a culture or religion. The hula dance of Hawaii is danced to poetic chants called *mele*. The hula has ancient religious ties and is used to express aspects of the mele (poetry), which can be prayers, love songs, or songs praising the land.

You may dance simply because you love it. If you pay attention while you dance, you may notice that you're using dance to express how you feel—happy, angry, excited, or sad. Perhaps you're taking dance lessons, like ballet or jazz. Maybe you've learned how to dance from members of your family as part of family traditions and get-togethers. Or maybe you just like to move and dance to your favorite music whenever you feel like it. Sometimes it's great just to move in whatever way you want when no one else is looking. No matter how you dance, if you enjoy it and feel comfortable doing it, you're Body Smart.

Like dance, creative activities such as mime, acting, and doing imitations take some Body Smart know-how. For example, you use your whole body when you act. Your posture, your movements, the way you hold your hands, the expression on your face—all of these body cues help create a character. Some actors literally use their bodies from their hair to their feet to express what the character is feeling. Comedians like Whoopi Goldberg, Robin Williams, and Jim Carrey use everything from a carefully raised eyebrow to twisting themselves up like a pretzel to make you laugh.

Mimes, like actors, also create a character. The characters they create can be graceful or bumbling, funny or sad. But they do more than just craft and develop a character. A mime makes that character react to objects in an invisible world that you see only through their finely coordinated movements. This is pretty difficult to do, since mimes don't speak and use few, if any, props.

Other artists have to be Body Smart, too. Musicians must learn how to use their fingers and mouths, and sometimes their entire bodies, to play an instrument. Painters and sculptors have to be able to use their bodies to show what their minds see. Painters need to move their brushes with care and control to get the effects they want. Sculptors may need to be very strong if they work with metal or stone.

> ### Did You Know?
>
> Actress Gwyneth Paltrow has received rave acting reviews—for her feet! The theatre critic for the *London Evening Standard* said this talented actress "manages to use her toes to express annoyance, frustration, unhappiness and a whole range of emotions that some actresses cannot manage with their faces, let alone their feet."

Using your body expressively can be a lot of fun, but it can also take a lot of practice. If you dance, you may practice the same moves over and over again in front of a mirror until they look and feel right. Actors, comedians, and mimes all spend their share of time in front of mirrors as well, getting to know their expressions and movements. (Jim Carrey used

A glass blower uses each part of her body to create a piece of blown glass—even a small one. She uses her arms and hands to hold the glass and move it while it melts. She uses her mouth and lungs to blow air carefully into the hot glass. She uses her shoulders and back to twirl the pipe the glass is formed on to expand the glass form.

to spend hours in front of a mirror when he was a kid, practicing silly faces, gestures, and movements.) You don't always have to stand in front of a mirror to do it, but it's well worth learning how to express yourself with your body, whether you do pliés or pratfalls, or whether you use your body to create beautiful sculptures or music.

EXERCISING YOUR BODY SMART BRAIN

Just as with many of the other intelligences, you can understand Body Smart better by using imagery. In fact, many people are able to think better by using physical, or *kinesthetic,* imagery. Close your eyes and imagine the situations below. Don't just picture them—actually try to imagine what each one really *feels* like in your body. What sensations does your body experience? Are you hot or cold? Wet or dry? Tense or relaxed? What are you smelling, seeing, hearing, touching, and even tasting?

* You're lifting a heavy weight.
* You're walking and slipping on a slick patch of ice.
* You're doing a double somersault off a diving board.
* You're slopping around in a barrel full of mud.
* You're swinging on the playground.
* You're riding the world's fastest roller coaster!

Were you able to sense the feelings in your body of lifting, slipping, and spinning around? Were you able to feel the mud between your toes, the breeze on your face as the swing goes back and forth, or the crazy twists and turns of the roller coaster as it speeds up and plummets down the hills? Those physical sensations you get in your imagination are examples of kinesthetic imagery or *body thinking.* Taking your body through these imaginary situations can help you be creative and even polish your problem-solving skills.

Many creative thinkers use body thinking in their work. Designers of chairs, couches, or the interiors of cars, for example, may use body thinking as they imagine how different shapes might feel to sit down on. This is another way your body can help you process information that can let you invent more interesting games, design more complicated science projects, or build a better mobile. Even athletes use this kind of thinking to improve their performances—whether they're gymnasts practicing their dismounts or basketball players practicing free throws.

You may find that your Body Smart self shines brightest when you use your abilities to physically create what you're thinking about. You might build a castle or spaceship you're writing about to help you figure out what you want your characters to do. Or you might make clay models of animals that you're learning about. You might construct a model of a house you want to build someday. (Architects usually build tiny mock-ups, or miniatures, of the homes and buildings they design on paper.)

You might also learn and process information through your five senses, especially through your sense of touch. You can get a lot of information about something just by touching it. You can figure out its shape, how many parts it has, or whether it's cold or hot, mushy or solid, smooth or rough. Learning through touch can develop something called *tactile sensitivity*. When you become more sensitive to touch in this way, you can figure out what things are without having to see them.

To practice your tactile sensitivity, you can create a collection of "favorite things to touch" with shapes and textures that you like. This could be anything from scraps of nice fabric (like velvet) to dried beans. Make a game out of your sense of touch—have someone put mystery objects into a box and then try to guess what they are by only feeling their

> ## Did You Know?
> Many athletes from ice skaters to gymnasts to field-goal kickers use kinesthetic (and even visual) imagery to help themselves practice their routines, nail their dismounts, or make a field goal. Using imagery also boosts their confidence, gets their bodies and their minds familiar with the moves, and helps them win.

shapes and textures. This can be a fun game around Halloween—use things like cooked spaghetti, gelatin, and frozen grapes to convince your friends that they're really touching creepy things like brains and eyeballs.

Did You Know?

Frank Lloyd Wright was one of America's most famous architects. He once said that his love of creating buildings first came from the feel of the plain wooden blocks that he played with when he was a child. His architect's mind started in his fingers.

You can learn a lot through your sense of touch (and all of your senses), but maybe you learn better when you move around. A lot of people simply like to move while they think. Walking or moving around helps them solve problems, learn, and explain things. You may notice that your teachers often think on their feet, answering your questions and explaining new ideas as they walk around the classroom.

You might find that your best ideas come to you when you're moving; it's easier for you to think when you're fiddling with something in your hands or walking, jogging, or hiking. If so, you're in good company. There are many creative and curious people who have found that movement helps them better focus their minds.

Sometimes it may be frustrating for Body Smart kids to learn in the traditional way: sitting at a desk, looking at a chalkboard, and listening to a teacher talk. Do you learn better while moving around or touching objects as you explore them? Some Body Smart kids may even be labeled hyperactive or told they have *attention deficit hyperactivity disorder* (ADHD). You might be one of those kids. If you like to move around a lot, need to build things in order to learn about them, or prefer lots of physical touch as you explore something new, then you might have been called hyperactive or ADHD yourself (or know someone who has).

This doesn't mean that if you have a lot of energy you're "hyper" or if you like to move around while you learn that you have a "learning disorder." But, you may be very Body Smart and end up with a label like ADHD. If so, you might feel confused, upset, or worried.

Part of the problem is that being called ADHD or hyper can keep everyone, including you, from seeing who you *really* are inside, how you learn, and what you do *best*. If you get into trouble at school, it might be because you have a lot of energy. Most schools don't have anything for you to do with all of that energy except go out for recess. And there's a lot more desk-time at school than there is recess. If you fidget, get bored easily, interrupt or talk while others are talking, and forget school tasks, then you and your teacher are probably both frustrated.

> ### Did You Know?
> Edwin Land got all of his best ideas while going on walks. What was one of his best ideas? One that you may be using today—instant photography and the Polaroid camera.

Whether you've got a label or not, talk with your parents and teachers about finding outlets for your energy. See if together you can think of new ways to use your Body Smart skills in and outside of school. Ask your teachers if they'll let you show what you've learned in different ways. Building models, acting in skits, or inventing things are all projects you might be able to do for school. Look for activities outside of school that help you focus and use your physical energy and curiosity. Getting involved in sports, dance classes, or acting are good ways to do this.

All that physical energy inside of you is a *good* thing if you use it in creative and useful ways. Remember that you're in good company. Some famous people who have been labeled as ADHD or hyperactive include actors and comedians Jim Carrey, Tracey Gold, and Bill Cosby, athletes Nolan Ryan and Michael Jordan, and movie director Steven Spielberg. By channeling their energy and their Body Smart abilities, these people succeeded in doing what they love. Along the way they've won awards, started charities, raised millions of dollars for important causes, and influenced the lives of countless people. Where will your energy take *you?*

Fun Ways to Become More Body Smart

Here are some ways that you can expand and enjoy your Body Smart skills. Try *any* activity that appeals to you no matter how Body Smart you think you are.

1 **Practice your hand-eye coordination.** Learn how to juggle, which is a great activity for getting your eyes, mind, and hands to work together. Other activities that develop this are playing marbles, jacks, Ping Pong, and video games. (All that work with the joystick really helps develop your reflexes!)

2 **Increase your hand-eye coordination through sports.** Shoot baskets, throw horseshoes or darts, or try bowling. Practice your tennis swing, volleyball serves, or batting skills.

3 **Get silly and get Body Smart.** Practice doing silly body tricks. Try to touch the tip of your tongue to the end of your nose. Figure out how to flare your nostrils or raise one eyebrow. Make weird sounds by cupping your hand in your underarm and moving your arm up and down. Practice wiggling your ears (it's really hard for some people!). Write your name on a piece of paper with your toes. (What other things can you do with your toes that you'd normally do with your fingers?)

4 **Play charades with family and friends.** Charades are a great way to express ideas using only your body. If you enjoy that game, try having a "conversation" with another person without using any words.

5 **Look for ideas while you move and exercise.** Keep a small notebook or tape recorder with you when you go on long walks or hikes, and write or sketch any interesting ideas you have. You might find yourself writing poems, solving math problems, or getting ideas for drawings.

6 **Learn how to give shoulder rubs to your friends and family.** Shoulder rubs feel good, and you learn how muscles work, what they feel like, and how tense they can get. Always make sure to ask before you give someone a shoulder rub and check to see that he or she is enjoying what you're doing. What feels good to one person might tickle or pinch someone else.

7 **Think of an idea and then *build it*.** Use clay, paperclips, papier-mâché, pipe cleaners, boxes, construction paper, or whatever other materials you may have around the house. You'll be stretching your mind as you stretch your fingers.

8 **Get fit.** Make your heart and lungs strong and improve your endurance by doing aerobic activities. Aerobic activities are things like dancing, running, jogging, speed walking, aerobics, or biking. Increase your physical strength by doing exercises such as push-ups, pull-ups, and sit-ups, or by working out with weights (with adult supervision). Do stretching exercises to warm up or cool down for your strength and aerobic activities and to get more flexible.

9 **Learn an art or a craft.** Explore things like: knitting, crochet, weaving (with paper or yarn), sewing, embroidery, needlepoint, beading, macramé, knot-tying, fly tying (for fishing), building models, or calligraphy (fancy and intricate handwriting). With adult supervision you might also explore carpentry, wood carving, cooking, or stained glass.

10 **Let your stress go and relax.** Learn ways to become more aware of your body and how to relax it when you're stressed out. Stress affects your body and your mind, so if you're worried about a test, your homework, or your family, it's time to find ways to de-stress. Take a relaxation tour of your body. Lie down and start breathing deeply. Starting with your toes, clench up your muscles and then relax them while you exhale. Continue to do this as you move up your body to your feet, your calves, and so on until you reach the top of your head. Yoga and tai chi are also good ways to de-stress. Letting go of stress helps you do better in school, sleep better, and feel better overall.

11 **Take a drama class or try out for a play.** You may have the chance in school to act in class skits or a school play. If you like acting, look for places in your community where you can try it such as community theater groups or even peer education groups that may do skits and plays on topics like getting along, drugs, and bullying.

12 **Take martial arts lessons.** There are many different kinds of martial arts. Some like aikido are purely defensive and teach you how to use your opponent's moves against them. Others like karate, jujitsu, or tae kwon do emphasize a more proactive approach and involve a lot of *sparring,* or practice fighting, in class to teach control and discipline. Visit different classes available in your community until you find one that you like and can afford. Community centers may be a good place to look for local classes.

13 **Focus on learning or becoming better at a sport you can do by yourself.** These solo sports include: swimming, running, archery, skateboarding, biking, skiing, or snowboarding. You might practice these with other people or compete on a team, but they are all activities that you can work on by yourself as well. Sports can help you get fit, make friends, and de-stress.

14 **Join a sports team in your neighborhood or at school.** If you like playing sports with others, look for opportunities at school or in your neighborhood. If you're a beginner, you might want to try intramural sports or neighborhood leagues. If you're looking for something more casual, get your friends together for pick-up games of basketball, baseball, roller hockey, volleyball, or soccer in your neighborhood. If you want to go for it and get serious about being competitive, try out for a competitive school team or a serious neighborhood team.

What If You Feel Out of Touch with the Body Smart You?

So maybe you trip over your own two feet or have trouble catching a ball without dropping it. (Or it seems that way sometimes.) You're still Body Smart. No matter what you're strongest in, *all* of your other intelligences rely on Body Smart skills. You couldn't write a great story without holding a pencil or tapping the keyboard with your fingers. You couldn't play the drums without coordinating your arms and legs.

You're using Body Smart skills all of the time whether you realize it or not. And you can always use the smarts you're strongest or most comfortable in to become more Body Smart.

Here are seven ways to do it:

 If you're Word Smart: Act out your favorite story or poem. Read stories about your favorite sports or activities, or read books and magazines to learn more and get hints about them. Practice your handwriting by writing out your favorite poems or quotes in your nicest script. Go for a walk and take a small notebook with you to write down story or poem ideas.

 If you're Music Smart: Exercise to music. Work on movement skills that use songs or create their own rhythms like jumping rope, jumping jacks, or even jogging.

 If you're Logic Smart: Try using your good sense of numbers and logic to figure out the best angles to throw a basketball, hit a baseball or tennis ball, or kick a soccer ball. Learn the rules to games you're curious about and figure out different strategies for playing them.

 If you're Picture Smart: Draw, paint, and sculpt. They all use Body Smart skills, so try experimenting. Paint or draw using big strokes, then little strokes. You probably haven't done any finger painting since you were younger, so give it another try. Grab some handfuls of color and really play with the feel of your painting. Mold clay to strengthen your hand muscles.

 If you're People Smart: Try different team sports like basketball, volleyball, or football. Intramural teams are a good way to meet people while developing your Body Smart skills. Or try skating, walking, dancing, or jogging with a friend. Including a friend may make these physical activities a lot more fun for you.

If you're Self Smart: Try solo sports like swimming or running. Once you become comfortable with a solo sport, you may find it offers a special time in your day to do something just for you.

 If you're Nature Smart: Take a walk or run in the woods or in your neighborhood. Listen to tapes of nature sounds while you dance, jump rope, or exercise in any way.

What If You're a Body Smart Big Shot?

When you're Body Smart, you can always become even better. If you play sports, try out for a school team. Or try a completely different sport—if you like volleyball, try basketball or biking. (Michael Jordan switched from basketball to baseball and actually played *professional* baseball for a year, just to try something that he'd always wanted to do.) Or do something really different to exercise those Body Smart abilities of yours. If you're good with your hands, use them to learn a musical instrument or use your entire body to learn a sport. Or get creative and experiment with using your body to express yourself through acting or dance.

Your Body Smart skills can help you build your other intelligences. Here are some Body Smart ideas you can use to help you understand and develop the other intelligences in school and in life.

 For Word Smart, get physical with your words. Write out your vocabulary or spelling words and trace over them with your finger. Or use word magnets you can move around to make up stories or write poetry.

 For Music Smart, use dance as a way to listen to and appreciate music. Notice the rhythms, patterns, and melodies that your body picks up on and moves to. Exercises like aerobics, which are usually done to music, also work really well.

For Logic Smart, try building something like a shelf, small bookcase, or box. You'll learn about different kinds of math by measuring the pieces and estimating the material you'll need. You'll even do some geometry, because you'll have to understand how certain kinds of angles work to make a structure strong.

 For Picture Smart, experiment with the feel and the sensations of different art materials. Modeling clay, making papier-mâché, painting with your hands and fingers (instead of a brush), and crayon rubbings are all good ways to play with the feel and texture of art while learning about drawing, shape, perspective, and color.

 For People Smart, learn magic tricks. Magic is more than just quick hands. A lot of magic is learning how people respond to it—how to distract them from the way you're doing the trick, entertain them while you're setting the trick up, and mislead them as to how the trick is done.

 For Self Smart, do activities that help you focus your mind and think about your day. Yoga and tai chi are good activities because they teach meditation as well as physical poses. (See pages 93–94 for more about them.) Sports that you do by yourself like running and biking are also good ways to create this thinking time.

 For Nature Smart, go on interactive or themed hikes or walks in your neighborhood. Go on a bird walk and look for as many different kinds of birds as possible. Or go on a leaf or flower walk, where you collect a variety of different kinds to dry and put in a scrapbook. Or if you live in the city, pick a shape or color and look for it in the buildings, sidewalks, signs, and cars. You'll start seeing things you never noticed before and may learn more about where you live.

Hey! Isn't that a blue-crowned, speckle-breasted nut wren... errr ... or something ...?

Look to the Future

What can you do with your Body Smart skills when you get older? A lot of very different things. Some of the careers you might look into include:

acrobat ▪ actor ▪ cabinet maker ▪ carpenter ▪ choreographer ▪ circus performer ▪ construction worker/builder ▪ cosmetologist ▪ craftsperson (examples: potter, glass blower, weaver, basket maker, and more) ▪ dancer ▪ dentist ▪ factory worker ▪ gymnast ▪ hair stylist ▪ handy person ▪ jeweler ▪ leather worker ▪ lifeguard ▪ magician ▪ massage therapist ▪ martial artist ▪ mechanic ▪ mime ▪ musician ▪ orchestra conductor ▪ physical education teacher ▪ physical therapist ▪ professional athlete ▪ sculptor ▪ stunt person ▪ surgeon ▪ tailor ▪ welder ▪ woodworker ▪ and many more!

Get Smart with These Resources

 ## Books and Magazines

The Bones Book & Skeleton by Stephen Cumbaa (New York: Workman, 1992). Put together and display a 12-inch, 25-piece skeleton, and learn about your own skeleton.

Grossology: The Science of Really Gross Things (Grossology Series) by Sylvia Branzei and Jack Keely (New York: Penguin, 1996). Icky but accurate, this fun book explains how your body works, covering everything from boogers to toe jam.

Kids Around the World Create! The Best Crafts and Activities from Many Lands by Arlette N. Braman (New York: John Wiley and Sons, 1999). Make Italian carnival masks, create Egyptian beaded jewelry, or weave Guatemalan-patterned bookmarks from a cardboard loom you make yourself. These crafts open the door to a world of fun.

The Klutz Book of Knots: How to Tie the World's 25 Most Useful Hitches, Ties, Wraps, and Knots by John Cassidy (Palo Alto, CA: Klutz, 1985). Like the title says, teach yourself a selection of the most useful knots around. Comes with color-coded nylon cord for practice in making knots.

Looking Inside Sports Aerodynamics by Ron Schultz (Santa Fe, NM: John Muir, 1992). Physics and sports? Find out how things like gravity, friction, and force play important roles in some of your favorite games and sports like baseball, football, basketball, and frisbee.

The Most Excellent Book of How to Be a Magician by Peter Eldin (Sussex, England: Copper Beech Publishing, 1996). Learn the nuts and bolts of conjuring using household materials for costumes and props. The instructions for the tricks are illustrated with color pictures and detailed drawings.

The New Way Things Work by David Macaulay (New York: Houghton Mifflin Company, 1998). Covering everything from zippers to computers, the author uses friendly language and colorful illustrations to show you how things work and why. (Macaulay has also written fun books on how different buildings—including pyramids, castles, and cathedrals—are built.)

The Right Moves to Getting Fit & Feeling Great! by Tina Schwager and Michele Schuerger (Minneapolis: Free Spirit Publishing, 1998). Filled with useful information on getting healthy and active, this book covers everything from eating well to creating a workout routine to profiles of different sports, and includes lots of helpful resources that are good for girls and boys alike.

Show Time: Music, Dance, and Drama Activities for Kids by Lisa Bany-Winters (Chicago: Chicago Review Press, 2000). With more than 80 activities, this book will have you creating a mirror dance, putting on plays and puppet shows, and acting out songs.

Sports Illustrated for Kids
www.sikids.com
This periodical includes regular sports features on athletes you know and new sports you may not. Also includes puzzles, games, photos, information on fantasy leagues, and more.

 Other

The Craftsman/NSTA Young Inventors Awards Program
www.nsta.org/programs/craftsman
In this contest for students in second through eighth grade, you invent and design a new tool that does something practical like fix things, make life easier, entertain, or solve a common problem. You build the tool under the guidance of an adult.

Web Sites

Building Big

www.pbs.org/wgbh/buildingbig

This Web site has all kinds of activities that let you experiment with building different structures including a dome, tunnel, and bridge, or fixing a dam or skyscrapers. This site also has interesting facts and information about big structures of all sorts, the people who build them, and how they do it.

Chapter 6

People Smart

Quick Quiz

Do you:

* like to people watch?
* make friends easily?
* offer to help when someone needs it?
* enjoy group activities and lively conversations?
* help other people around you get along better?
* feel confident when meeting new people?
* like to organize activities for you and your friends?
* easily guess how people are feeling just by looking at them?
* know how to get people excited about working together or how to get them involved in things you're interested in?
* prefer to work and learn with others rather than alone?
* enjoy getting people to see things your way?
* get concerned about issues of fairness and right and wrong?
* enjoy volunteering for causes that help other people?

If you answered yes to any of the questions above, then you just identified some of the ways you're People Smart!

What Does It Mean to Be People Smart?

You like people and can express it in an amazing number of ways. On a basic level, you enjoy working, learning, helping, and being with other people. You may have a very good natural understanding of how people are feeling, what they want or need, and why they do what they do. You may enjoy making friends or work well in social groups of all different kinds. If you're People Smart, you could show it by leading a club or school organization, having lots of friends, helping other people get along, inspiring others to get involved in a cause, or organizing activities for your family or friends.

Being People Smart also means that you genuinely care about people and enjoy finding ways to help them. This might mean that you understand and are nice to the shy or less well-liked kids in school. Or it can mean that you're good at resolving arguments between your friends or siblings. You may like volunteering to help people directly (for example, shoveling snow off an elderly neighbor's sidewalk) or through service organizations (like the local food bank). If it sounds like there are a lot of ways to be People Smart, it's because there are. But one of the most important People Smart abilities you can have is *understanding others.*

You know that people read books—but did you know that people can also read *people?* When you smile at someone, that person "reads" your face and guesses that you're happy; if you frown, you send the message that you're sad or upset. But reading books can sometimes be much easier than reading people.

For example, there are lots of different *kinds* of smiles. A big grin might say: "I'm happy to see you!" A tight smile could say: "I'm angry at you, but I don't want you to

Did You Know?

Scientists estimate that there are over 700,000 different things we can do with our faces, gestures, and body postures to communicate. With so many ways to communicate before we even open our mouths, it's impressive that we can understand each other at all!

know it." A fake-looking smile might say: "I'm uncomfortable meeting you, but I have to be polite and smile like this anyway!" It takes intelligence to tell the difference between these kinds of smiles. It takes People Smart.

Experts in social science say that within a few seconds of meeting another person, before you even start speaking, both of you have sized each other up *without using words.* So in the time that it might take you to sneeze, each of you have read a bunch of social signals and made some decisions about how you feel about each other! That's pretty amazing, and you do it every day in school, at home, and everywhere you go. Sizing someone up this way can help you decide if the person makes you feel uncomfortable or has the potential to become a friend.

Some kids are good at reading people. (Maybe you're one of them.) They can stand in a crowd or classroom and tell you which kids like each other and which kids don't. A good "people reader" may be able to quickly pick out the cliques or friendship groups, or figure out who has a crush on who, or point out which kids tend to get picked on. And he or she can do all of this just by looking at things like winks, glances, taps, facial expressions, and postures (how people stand, sit, or position their bodies). Sometime today try reading the people around you. You might be surprised at how much everyone's saying *without ever saying a word!*

Suppose you run into someone who isn't good at reading expressions or gestures. Maybe you have a bored look on your face, but the person misreads you and thinks you're angry. Or maybe you give someone a friendly tap on the shoulder, but the person thinks you're being rude. See how easy it can be to misinterpret another person's meaning?

Because a big part of being People Smart is the ability to read other people, you can probably see how important this intelligence is in all the different areas of your life. Being able to read people helps you communicate

Did You Know?

There are different kinds of body "languages." Depending on what culture or country you're in, the same gesture or expression can have very different meanings. For example, in America, bowing is something people usually do onstage after a play or a concert. In Japan, bowing is an everyday occurrence and people may bow when they greet each other as a sign of respect.

and get along with them. You may be more successful in your life because you're able to understand what other people need and how to get what you need from them—for example, help on your math homework or money when you're collecting for a good cause. Being able to read people can help you give them what they need, too.

One expert in People Smart, a psychologist named Daniel Goleman, says that the business world is often made up of people with lower IQ scores who are in charge of people with higher IQ scores. (For more about IQ, see pages 1–2.) So the people in charge didn't necessarily get the highest test scores or the best grades, but they often end up leading the people who *did*. Does this surprise you?

Take a moment to think about the kids at your school who are commonly thought of as the most "popular." Are they the brightest students? Are they the leaders in student government? Or are they popular for different reasons, such as their confidence, charm, compassion, or personality? Many People Smart kids are popular among students and teachers because they know how to get along with others—not because they get A's in every class (although some do).

This doesn't mean you can't be a good leader *and* be smart in other areas, too. You can be strong in any and all of the eight intelligences and still do well in school, have close friends, and be popular. And just because you're smart in math or good at writing poetry (for example), this doesn't mean that people are a mystery to you. You can be People Smart and any other smart at the same time!

What can being People Smart do for you?

* It can help you get along with others, including your friends, parents, siblings, classmates, and teammates.

* It can help you make friends.

* You can use it to solve disputes and help others get along better.

* You can use it to organize and lead people.

Things you may do every day that use this intelligence:
hang out with friends ▪ volunteer to help people ▪ make friends ▪ help your friends or siblings resolve conflicts ▪ study in groups or work on group projects ▪ play team sports ▪ tutor classmates or siblings ▪ work in class with other students ▪ sell things for school or organization fundraisers ▪ organize activities for you and your friends ▪ throw a party or get together with friends ▪ talk on the phone with your friends ▪ send email to people you know ▪ play games with people ▪ people watch

REACHING OUT

The most basic part of being People Smart is understanding people and reaching out to them. You do this every day and probably don't even realize it.

One of the most common—and best—ways you can use your People Smart abilities is to make friends. You can be People Smart simply by having friends and enjoying their company whether you play games or sports, go to the movies, or just talk. You can be People Smart when you have lots of friends and everyone in the neighborhood knows your name or if you have only a few friends who you're close to and enjoy spending time with.

Friendships are important, and being People Smart can help you make and keep friends. If you want more friends or if you feel lonely, there are some easy ways to boost your People Smart skills and use them to make new friends. Here are some simple tips for becoming more of a "people person":

* **Smile!** It's a simple thing, but when you smile at people, you're letting them know you like them and are interested in them. People are more likely to respond positively to you when you smile.

* **Listen.** Give your new friends plenty of time to talk, and focus on what they're saying. Don't hog the conversation or interrupt. Even if you're really excited by what they're saying, let them finish talking before you respond. You can practice *active listening*, which

means paying close attention to what someone is saying *and* letting the person know it by smiling, nodding, saying "uh-huh," or asking questions.

* **Be yourself.** If you're shy or don't feel comfortable talking a lot, you can still show your People Smarts. If you ask good questions and pay attention to the answers, you're already opening the door to friendship. (Think about talk-show hosts like Oprah Winfrey— they ask careful questions and then do a lot of listening. Many talk-show hosts don't talk as much as you may think!)

* **Find shared interests.** When you're talking, find topics that appeal to both you and the other person. Common interests help you get to know someone, and they keep the conversation going.

* **Put the odds in your favor.** Go where there are people who share your interests. So if you like stamp collecting, find a group of stamp collectors. If you're a soccer fan, join the soccer team. If you love to read, join a book club.

Reaching out to others isn't always easy—it can take a bit of "people courage" to do it. But the more you work at making friends, the better you'll get. It takes practice, just like riding a bicycle or learning to play the violin. If you don't make friends every time you try, that's okay. At least you made the effort and opened yourself up to new experiences—and that's important, too.

All these open doors might lead you to make friends with people you never would have thought of reaching out to before. You might become friends with people from different cultures, religions, and countries, or just different neighborhoods and schools. Or you could make friends with someone older or younger. With every new friend you make, the world becomes a smaller place and your home in it grows a little larger.

HELPING OUT

You can take your People Smart abilities a step further and use them to help people. Get involved in volunteer work and service to others. You might work for a local service organization (for example, reading to younger kids in a local Head Start program), or you might give your time to an international cause (like writing letters for Amnesty International, an organization that works for human rights around the world). Perhaps you'll choose to work with kids your own age to help them get along better. No matter how you decide to use your People Smart skills to help others, you can make a huge difference.

The reason you may want to help other people is because you have something called *empathy*. When you have empathy, you're sensitive to other people's problems, feelings, and experiences. In other words, you're able to put yourself in another person's shoes and imagine what it's like to walk in those shoes. Empathy is why you may try to be friends with the shyest kid in your class or stand up to a school bully for someone else. It's also the reason you may raise money for UNICEF (the United Nations International Children's Emergency Fund) or help serve Thanksgiving dinner at a local homeless shelter.

When you start volunteering your time to help others, you might be amazed at the number of different things you can do. You could organize a food drive at your school for a local food bank, visit senior citizens, or volunteer at the Special Olympics. Or you might want to help other kids in your school, neighborhood, or community.

One 11-year-old girl named Aubyn C. Burnside started a program in 1996 called Suitcases for Kids. She'd found out that foster kids (or kids who are unable to live with the families they were born in or adopted to) often have to move around a lot. And when they move from foster home to foster home, they usually have to carry everything they own in whatever they can find—even paper bags or trash bags. Aubyn thought the foster kids would feel better about moving if they could pack their belongings in suitcases instead. She wrote a flyer and started getting

Did You Know?

UNICEF helps kids all over the world. UNICEF (the United Nations International Children's Emergency Fund) was created by the United Nations General Assembly in 1946. At first it was used to help all the children who were in need—orphaned, homeless, hungry—in Europe after World War II. In 1953, it became a permanent part of the United Nations with a goal of helping children all over the world. UNICEF's mission includes education, children's health, and protecting children who live in war-torn areas.

people to donate their old suitcases, which she then gave to her local social services office to give to foster kids. Today Suitcases for Kids has spread to 49 states and Canada—all because an 11-year-old used her People Smart abilities. You can make a real difference in other people's lives, too!

Social action and service can use any of your intelligences depending on what you're interested in and how you decide to help. You can use Word Smart know-how to teach people to read, or your Nature Smart skills when you rally your classmates and friends to help clean up a local park. There are a lot of possibilities. Here are some ideas you might try:

* Help classmates who are learning English as a second language with their homework.

* Organize and donate to a coat and mitten drive for families in need.

* Do yard work or run errands for an ill or elderly neighbor.

* Organize a safe walking program to help younger children get to and from school or bus stops.

* Volunteer to give after-school lessons in music, art, or dance.

* Collect stuffed animals and toys for a children's hospital.

You can also use your People Smart skills by being a *mediator*, or someone who resolves conflicts and helps others get along better. When an argument or fight breaks out in your school or neighborhood, do you notice how there's often one kid who jumps in to try to resolve the disagreement? (Maybe that kid is you!) Some kids are very good at this—they have a knack for resolving conflicts or arguments, for calming people down, for getting people to listen to each other, or at least for convincing them to stop fighting and go home! When you put all of these things together, you a have a very important People Smart ability—*conflict resolution*.

Conflict resolution is such an important part of being People Smart because daily life can be filled with disagreements, arguments, and plain old misunderstandings. Even when people make their best efforts to get along, problems may come up. (And there are times when people don't even *try* to get along.) Whenever a conflict breaks out, it helps to have someone around who can help solve the problem.

Maybe *you're* good at resolving conflicts and solving problems between your friends or classmates. (When you grow up, you might end up solving conflicts between people, organizations, or even countries!) You can practice your skills right now if your school has a conflict resolution or peer mediation program to help with problems that come up between students. Or you might want to become a peer counselor. Peer counselors help other students by answering questions and giving advice and support to classmates who are having problems. Those problems can be anything from getting along with others to bullying to school stress to trouble at home. Find out what kind of program your school has and how you can get involved.

Another important People Smart skill is called *negotiation*. When you negotiate with someone, you try to understand what he or she wants, and compare that with what *you* want, and then try to meet both your needs. If this doesn't happen, then you need to negotiate— being willing to change what you want and getting the other person to change what he or she wants, so you can both get as much of what you *really* want as possible.

For example, maybe you're at home and about to sit down to watch your favorite television show. Your sister wants to watch *her* favorite TV show on another channel. This could turn into a big fight unless you know how to negotiate. You might say: "Let me watch this show, and I'll let you borrow my skateboard for a week." Or you might try: "Okay, I'll let you watch your show today if you clean up my room for me." Neither of these suggestions may do the trick, but if you're good at negotiating, then you can probably

> ## Did You Know?
> Former U.S. President Jimmy Carter won a Nobel Peace Prize in 2002 for his skills at conflict resolution and negotiation. He has worked all over the world, including in the United States, for peace and human rights issues.

find something to offer or something to give up in order to get what you both want. When both people end up happy and avoid conflict, it's called a "win-win" situation—and that's a smart choice.

LEADING THE WAY

The ability to lead people is another way of being People Smart. What makes someone a good leader? A person who understands and cares about others. Good leaders have other traits in common as well:

* confidence (they believe in themselves and in the people they're leading)

* a knack for grabbing people's attention and getting them interested in a common idea, cause, or goal

* a certain comfort level with being in the spotlight

* a desire to work with others to create change

* the ability to get people to work together and cooperate

* a willingness to take risks and dream big

What trait don't you see on this list? *Age.* You can be a good leader at almost any age. People who grow into good leaders often show these traits at an early age and continue to develop them throughout their lives.

There are examples of leadership everywhere you turn. Parents lead their families; teachers lead in the classroom; principals lead entire schools. Nations may be led by presidents or prime ministers. There are probably leaders your own age all around you: the class president, team captains, leaders of school clubs, youth groups leaders. Have you ever thought about being a leader—or are you already? In what part of your life? (At school? In a club? While doing volunteer work?) What does leadership mean to you?

If you're interested in developing your leadership skills, you can start by taking more responsibility in different areas of your life. When you do this, you're asking for the opportunity to do something instead of waiting to be asked. Taking responsibility can mean different things: starting a study group, helping your teammates get along better, or organizing your friends to work on a community service project. You may find that the more important something is to you (your soccer team, your local park, helping the homeless), the more eager you are to get involved and start leading the way.

If you prefer to lead from behind the scenes instead of out in the spotlight, can you still be a leader? The answer is yes. Leadership is about working with other people to get things done, not about being out in front of the group. (You could be the person who keeps a study group on track, for example, without being the person who makes the group's presentation to the class.) Maybe you like to help people cooperate, smooth over their conflicts, and build on their strengths—all signs of a good leader. You might be the kind of People Smart person who quietly but positively brings out the best in all of your friends, classmates, and family members.

You can also be a leader by setting a strong example for others or by becoming a role model. Mattie Stepanek, an 11-year-old boy with a rare form of Muscular Dystrophy, became a leader this way. He started writing poems at the age of 3 to help himself understand and deal with his disease. His poems were published in two books, *Heartsongs* and *Journey Through Heartsongs,* and his message is one of courage, hope, and peace. His books have become best-sellers because kids and adults alike see him as a role model, a leader, and even a peacemaker.

Good leadership starts with the desire to reach out to others and help them in some way. Being a leader isn't about being bossy, it's about working to make a positive difference in the world around you.

Fun Ways to Become More People Smart

Here are some ways that you can expand and enjoy your People Smart skills. Try *any* activity that appeals to you no matter how People Smart you think you are.

1 **Start your own address book.** Keep a list of your friends and their phone numbers, addresses, and email addresses. Use this information to stay in touch. Even if you don't have anything particular to say, a quick note saying you're thinking of someone can mean a lot!

2 **Make your own social map.** Write your name in the middle of a piece of paper. Closest to your name, write the names of the people you are closest to (friends and family). Then write the names of friends and acquaintances who are not as close—put them as far from your name on the page as you feel connected to them (if you feel really distant from someone, put them on the edge of the page). Put as many names of people who you're friendly with as possible. Then look at the list. If you'd like more names on the page or you'd like the names to be closer to your name, practice the tips for making friends listed earlier in this chapter.

3 **Meet new people.** Decide to meet a new person each day, each week, or each month (you decide how many new people you want to meet). Start today: Introduce yourself to someone you'd like to know.

4 **Practice people watching.** Go to a public place—the playground, a grocery store, a mall—with a friend or family member. See how well the two of you can read the people around you. Look at their body language, the expressions on their faces (happy, sad, grumpy, tired), and how they're holding their bodies (do they stand up straight or slump?). Do they gesture or move their hands when they talk? What kind of nonverbal communication do you see (for example, shaking hands, touching someone lightly on the shoulder, or kissing)? Talk about what you saw and what you think it meant.

5 **Find "like minds."** Start a club or group that involves something you're interested in (examples: coins, books, nature, baseball, cooking, shopping, model-building). It's fun to spend time with people who enjoy the same things you do. You can work on projects together, think up new ideas, or just hang out. When you share common activities, you'll hardly ever run out of things to talk about.

6 **Volunteer to help others.** There are many different kinds of organizations that help people locally and globally. Some organizations you might consider getting involved with or volunteering for include the Red Cross, the Sierra Club, Future Farmers of America, UNICEF, and Amnesty International.

7 **Learn with others.** Make the most of group learning activities in your classroom—you can learn different ways to solve problems, hear different ideas, and get to know your classmates better. Find ways to study and learn with others outside of school—have homework sessions with friends, work on group art projects, or perform music with others. Ask your teachers to give the class more ways to learn and study in groups.

8 **Get involved.** Run for election in student government, volunteer to be part of your school's conflict resolution program, or look for other ways you can use your People Smart skills to help others at school.

9 **Tutor someone.** Offer to teach or tutor another student at school, or to serve as a "buddy" to a younger child. You'll feel good about helping someone, and you can brush up on your people skills.

10 **Spend time with your family.** Make a point of spending "quality" time with your family regularly to stay connected. You can have family meetings, where the family gets together to talk about important issues like chores, getting along, or expectations for school. Or you can have a family game night— play cards or board games, shoot hoops in the park, or even go bowling.

11 **Explore being a leader.** Whether you're a natural leader or generally prefer being a team player, explore what leadership means. Many organizations and volunteer groups have opportunities for you to try out your leadership capabilities. Some of them may have training or mentoring opportunities to help you learn leadership skills.

12 **Get a mentor.** A mentor is someone who can help you learn new skills and grow as a person. A mentor can act as a positive role model for you, help you grow more confident, help you meet other people with your interests, and encourage you to develop your leadership skills. You can find mentors in a lot of different places. A Scout or club leader, a leader at your place of worship, your coach, a family friend, a local business person, or someone who works at an organization where you volunteer could be a possible mentor.

13 **Look everywhere for learning opportunities.** Maybe you've never thought about it, but every person you meet (a) knows things you don't know yet, (b) has met people you've never met, and (c) has had experiences you've never had. Think about how much you can learn from that person! Reach out to new people and ask them lots of questions. At the end of each day, think about all the different people you met and ask yourself: "What did I learn from that person?"

14 **Look past labels.** It can be easy to carry around ideas about people without getting to know them. Maybe you've caught yourself thinking, "That person is such a nerd (loser, brain)." Instead of labeling people too quickly, find out what you may have in common with them or what they can teach you. You may not end up as friends, but at least you'll have made the effort to get to know them better. And if you do end up friends . . . wonderful!

15 **Practice making friends.** If you feel shy or awkward, practice making friends with someone you already know like a family member or an old friend. (Look at pages 115–116 for tips on how to make friends.) Making friends gets easier with practice. Pen pals can also be a fun way to get to know new people.

What If You Need to Polish Your People Smart Skills?

You may not realize it, but you already have People Smart abilities that you use every day at school and at home. Whenever you work, talk, share, and learn with others, you're being People Smart. (It's probably hard for you to think of a day when you don't do any of those things!) Even if you're shy or quiet, or if you feel awkward around new people, you may have hidden People Smart skills. Maybe you just need to uncover and polish up those skills so you feel more confident about them.

And you can always use the smarts you're strongest or most comfortable in to become more People Smart.

Here are seven ways to do it:

 If you're Word Smart: start sharing your words and ideas with others. Debating and writing speeches for class presentations or causes you support is one way to get started. Writing plays and skits and getting others to help perform them is another way. Take it a step further and get together with your Picture Smart friends and make cartoons and movies. Borrow a video camera or use a computer program and watch your stories come to life. Start a writing group with friends or classmates and share and comment on each other's stories and poetry.

 If you're Music Smart: Join (or start!) a choir or band and experience the fun of making music with others. Schools, community centers, and places of worship are all good places to look for music groups to get involved with. Share your favorite music with your friends and family, and ask them to share theirs with you. Go to concerts with others—high school or college bands, concerts in the park, even libraries sometimes sponsor concerts.

 If you're Logic Smart: Join or start a math review or study group. Get books of brainteasers, riddles, or puzzles and solve them with friends, classmates, or family members. Create logic puzzles and have others solve them—discuss their (and your) solutions. Get together with a friend or friends and conduct science experiments together.

 If you're Picture Smart: Look for ways you can make art with others. Group projects like painting a mural, putting together a collage, building sculptures or mobiles, or making a movie or a cartoon with your friends using a computer are great ways to be creative with other people. Share your love of art by teaching others how to draw or paint or make things from clay. Or explore different kinds of art and people by taking a community art class. Work on jigsaw puzzles or 3-D puzzles with your friends for fun.

If you're Body Smart: Join a team to play sports. Or you could join an athletic group or club and make friends while you learn a new sport or activity. Get a workout partner and have fun talking while you run, bicycle, or dance. Look for fun things to do with your friends like playing a game of tag, going swimming at a pool (or beach or lake), or practicing juggling together—you get to be social *and* get fit at the same time!

If you're Self Smart: Think about what you love doing the most—reading, singing, drawing, playing sports, or whatever. Next, think about how you can start doing this activity in a group or on a team, if you don't already. Sharing your interests with others is a great way to reach out and find new friends.

If you're Nature Smart: Did you know you can connect to people through your connection to the earth? Bring others to outdoor places you've discovered and enjoy. Get friends, classmates, and family members involved in group projects to clean up, protect, or beautify areas where you live. Get involved in a community garden. (You can even grow food for a good cause—give your home-grown vegetables, herbs, and fruit to a food bank or homeless shelter.)

What If You're a People Smart Powerhouse?

Maybe you love people and can't get enough of hanging out with them and helping them. Lucky you! But you can still find new ways to become more People Smart.

If you get along well with just about everybody, there are fun ways to show and share what you know. For example, join a peer mediation program so you can help people cooperate and get along. If there's an issue that's important to you, don't just talk about it—do something about it by getting other people involved and working together to make a difference.

If you love organizing your friends for worthy causes, try your hand at organizing on a larger level—your school, your community center, your place of worship. Your People Smart skills hold a world of possibilities.

Your People Smart skills can help you build your other intelligences. Here are some People Smart ideas you can use to help you understand and develop the other intelligences in school and in life.

 For Word Smart, practice your vocabulary and spelling words with your friends and family. Talk about the books you're reading with friends, family, and classmates, or even set up a book group to discuss books in-depth. Practice your reading by reading plays (especially out loud and with friends) and figure out why all the different characters are doing what they're doing.

 For Music Smart, listen to music with your friends and family and talk about what you hear. Talk with your friends and family about what kinds of music they like and why. Volunteer at a local arts organization and use the opportunity to learn more about different kinds of music—classical, opera, musical theatre.

 For Logic Smart, play math games with your friends. Find problems and puzzles to solve in groups. Start a math or science study group. Quiz your friends on math and science facts and have them quiz you.

 For Picture Smart, take art classes with your friends in school or through a community center. Get to know new people in the art class and get together to practice art outside of class or work on group projects like collages or murals. Offer to draw portraits of your friends. Start a craft club and get people to join. The club could sell its crafts to raise funds for a worthy cause.

 For Body Smart, learn new activities that you can do with others. Take a dance or martial arts class or join an intramural volleyball team. Go for walks, runs, and bike rides with your friends. If you play on a sports team, notice the People Smart skills that the team captain and the coach use to inspire you and the other players to play your best.

 For Self Smart, make a list of what you think your strongest People Smart skills are and the areas you think you need to work on. Using your list, think of three goals for improving the areas you want to work on. For example, you may decide you're pretty good at making friends and getting along with others, but you'd like to improve your leadership skills. Your three goals might look like this: (1) find a mentor to help me work on my leadership skills, (2) check to see if my school, the Scouts, or a community youth club have programs to help me develop leadership skills, (3) look for opportunities to practice leading—organizing others for volunteer work, running for student government.

 For Nature Smart, get involved with an environmental cause that really matters to you. It could be saving the sea otters or protecting local wetlands so that migrating birds have places to stopover. You can talk with people to raise their awareness, get signatures on petitions, or organize others. You can learn a lot about nature by working with others to protect it.

Look to the Future

So what can you do with your People Smart when you get older? A lot of very different things. Some of the careers you might look into include:

administrator ▪ advertising executive ▪ anthropologist ▪ arbitrator ▪ business leader ▪ business owner ▪ coach ▪ counselor ▪ criminologist ▪ home-care provider ▪ human resources specialist ▪ interviewer ▪ lawyer ▪ manager ▪ mediator ▪ nurse ▪ office manager ▪ personnel worker ▪ police officer ▪ politician ▪ pollster ▪ psychiatrist ▪ psychologist ▪ public relations specialist ▪ public speaker ▪ publicist ▪ receptionist ▪ reporter ▪ retail manager ▪ retail worker ▪ salesperson ▪ school principal ▪ social activist ▪ social director ▪ social worker ▪ sociologist ▪ talk-show host ▪ teacher ▪ therapist ▪ travel agent ▪ waitress/waiter ▪ and many more!

Get Smart with These Resources

 Books

Being Your Best: Character Building for Kids 7–10 by Barbara A. Lewis (Minneapolis: Free Spirit Publishing, 2000). A tool for building character traits like citizenship, fairness, respect, and responsibility, this book offers inspiring quotations, definitions, and background information on the important values that we all need to show each day. Find resources for making a difference at home, at school, and in the community.

Climbing Your Family Tree: Online and Off-Line Genealogy for Kids by Ira Wolfman (New York: Workman, 2001). A comprehensive and friendly primer on genealogy in the

21st century. Learn how to track down important family documents, create oral histories, make scrapbooks, and compile a family tree. Includes genealogical stories from other kids and a full chapter on online searching

The Kid's Guide to Service Projects: Over 500 Service Ideas for Young People Who Want to Make a Difference by Barbara A. Lewis (Minneapolis: Free Spirit Publishing, 1995). This book is full of great ideas for helping out in your community and making a difference in the world. From simple projects to large-scale commitments, this book provides you with the information you need to make a positive impact on the environment, hunger, politics, and more. Learn how to create flyers, petitions, press releases, and other effective materials for solving problems and getting things done.

The Kid's Guide to Social Action: How to Solve the Social Problems You Choose—and Turn Creative Thinking into Positive Action by Barbara A. Lewis (Minneapolis: Free Spirit Publishing, 1998). This book is a great hands-on tool for tackling the problems that you really care about. Discover how to write letters, make speeches, take surveys, and more. Resources include organizations, Web sites, and books that you can turn to for more help reaching your goal.

Psychology for Kids II: 40 Fun Experiments That Help You Learn About Others by Jonni Kincher (Minneapolis: Free Spirit Publishing, 1995). Based on science and real psychology, these experiments make it fun and interesting to learn about your family, friends, and classmates.

 Organizations

American Red Cross
2025 E Street NW
Washington, DC 20006
(202) 303-4498
www.redcross.org
This organization helps people around the world in emergency situations—from providing blood in medical emergencies to helping natural disaster victims by providing food and supplies, emotional support, and medical services. They collect donations of food, clothes, and blankets, and their work depends on volunteers. Contact them to find out for how to volunteer in your area.

America's Second Harvest
35 East Wacker Drive, #2000
Chicago, IL 60601
1-800-771-2303
www.secondharvest.org
This organization is the nation's largest network for feeding the hungry in the United States. It provides food to more than 23 million hungry Americans each year through more than 200 food banks and food-rescue programs. Contact them to find out where a food bank is near you and how you can help.

Amnesty International-USA/AI Kids
322 Eighth Avenue
New York, NY 10001
(212) 807-8400
www.amnesty-usa.org/aikids
Amnesty International, a leading human rights organization, has created AI Kids, an activist network for kids. It has information about Amnesty International, what human rights are, how kids can advocate for prisoners of conscience through letter writing, how to write polite letters to international figures, and a list of kids and teens around the world to write for.

Suitcases for Kids
P.O. Box 1144
Hickory, NC 28603
www.suitcasesforkids.org
This organization provides luggage to foster children, who often have to move between many homes or shelters. Contact them or visit their Web site for information on where you can donate and tips on how to start a suitcases-for-kids program in your area. (See pages 117–118 to read more about this organization.)

UNICEF
3 United Nations Plaza
New York, NY 10017
(212) 326-7000
www.unicef.org/young
UNICEF works with governments and other organizations to support young people around the world, providing services and supplies to children affected by illness, war, and natural disaster. Contact them or visit the above Web site to learn more about the issues facing children around the world and to discover how you can help.

 Web Sites

Do Something
www.dosomething.org
Learn about how you can help others while building strong relationships with peers.

Chapter 7

Self Smart

Quick Quiz

Do you:

* prefer to work on your own rather than with others?
* like to set and meet your own goals?
* stand up for your beliefs, even if they're not popular?
* worry less about what other people think of you than most kids?
* know how you're feeling and why most of the time?
* spend time thinking deeply about things that matter to you?
* have a strong sense of what you're good at and not so good at?
* enjoy keeping a diary or writing in your journal?
* write about your ideas, memories, feelings, or personal history?
* have a good sense of who you are?
* think about the future and what you'd like to be someday?

If you answered yes to any of the questions above, then you just identified some of the ways you're Self Smart!

What Does It Mean to Be Self Smart?

When you're Self Smart, you know yourself. You've got a good idea of who you are and what you can do. You're aware of your feelings, and you may understand yourself better than others understand you. You're able to set personal goals, think about and learn from your past experiences, and understand your strengths and weaknesses. You can show this intelligence by keeping a journal, working through problems in your life, creating a plan for the future, spending time regularly reflecting on your life, having an interest in religion or psychology, or being able to understand and accept the different sorts of feelings that come up inside of you every day.

Have you ever thought about who you really are? If someone asks "Who are you?" you might answer: "I'm John Doe" or "I'm Jane Doe." (Of course, you'd put your name in the answer—unless your name really *is* John or Jane Doe.) But that's just your *name*. You're certainly more than your name. You might go on to say: "Well, I'm 11 years old, and I live in San Jose, California, and I'm in sixth grade, and I love to play soccer." (Again, put in the answers that are true for you.) That may say a little bit more about you, but there's still a lot more to know.

There's more to you than just your age, the place where you live, your grade level, and the things you love to do. What about your past experiences, your hopes for the future, all your likes and dislikes, and your feelings? The more you describe yourself, the more you discover who you really are. *You* know more about yourself than anybody else. And knowing yourself well is what it means to be Self Smart.

You might think, "Everybody knows who they are, don't they?" Actually, not all people do. Some people are a lot more in touch with their personal feelings, goals, and dreams than others. Since Self Smart people know themselves well, they're better able to make smart choices in life. In fact, they may not be as influenced by peer pressure because they don't care as much about what other people think of them and don't want to do things that may interfere with reaching their goals.

Remember John and Jane Doe? Well, here are two examples of them using their Self Smart skills:

Jane's best friend really wants to try out for the school musical, but she doesn't want to do it alone and begs Jane to try out, too. After all, Jane has a good singing voice. But Jane says she doesn't want to try out because she knows she feels too nervous when she sings in front of a crowd; besides, she wants to use her after-school time to improve her soccer game instead. Jane knows what's best for her and doesn't give in to pressure from her friend. But she says she would be glad to watch the tryouts with her friend and cheer her on.

John's friends have been picking on a kid on the playground because he isn't very good at sports and is kind of shy. John's friends have started teasing John because he won't join them. In fact, John has started standing up for the kid his friends are bullying because he doesn't think what they're doing is right. Even though he knows his friends might not want to hang out with him, John decides to do what he thinks is right.

So, how are Jane and John being Self Smart? Jane recognizes her strengths (her soccer and her voice), her weaknesses (her fear of performing), and her goals (her desire to improve her soccer game). And she resists pressure from someone else to do what she doesn't feel is right for her. John stands up for what he believes in even though it could make him unpopular with his friends and gets him teased.

As you can see, Self Smart is about self-knowledge. And this is one of the most important kinds of knowledge to have. It may be hard to believe that knowing yourself can be more important than knowing how to do math problems, for example, or how to read music—but it's true. In fact, being Self Smart is an important key to living a successful life. When you know who you are and what you want your future to be like, you're more able to accomplish the things you set out to do. There's another bonus: When you're Self Smart, you can more easily build your other intelligences, too!

What can being Self Smart do for you?

* You can use it to learn from your mistakes and your successes, so you can make the most of all your intelligences.

* You can set goals for your future and learn from your past.

* You can understand your feelings and express them in healthy ways.

Things you may do every day that use this intelligence:

keep a journal ▪ make lists of things you really like (or really dislike) ▪ set goals for yourself, like getting your homework done before 6 P.M. or learning to play an instrument ▪ imagine your future job, home, or accomplishments ▪ daydream about the way you want your life to be ▪ think about or reflect on your day ▪ consider ways to become a better person ▪ read self-help books or self-improvement magazines ▪ take personality quizzes ▪ think and write about your dreams ▪ take care of yourself through healthy eating, exercise, and good hygiene

KNOWING YOURSELF

So, by now you probably get the idea that "knowing yourself" is important. But maybe it's still a mystery to you what this really means. How do you start getting to know yourself if it's something you haven't thought a lot about? And how can you know yourself when you're at an age when you're growing and changing so much?

Well, self-knowledge is an ongoing challenge—but that's what makes it so fun! Getting to know yourself is about exploring who you are—what you like, what you dislike, what you want, what you feel, what you believe in, what you stand for, and what you think you can give to the world. As you grow, have new experiences, and learn new things, you'll keep changing inside and out. It can be a lot to figure out, even for adults. That's why developing your Self Smart abilities takes time—but you're young and you've got lots of time to do it!

Self-knowledge starts with *self-evaluation*. And that means taking a good, hard look at yourself and your life. Ask yourself questions like these:

* What are my best qualities?
* What's going well for me? Where can I improve?
* What are my hopes and dreams?
* What makes me happy?
* What do I really want to learn?
* What goals do I have for my life right now?
* What are my goals for the future?
* What have I learned from my past?
* How do I feel right now? Why?
* How do I express my feelings?
* What do I believe in? Why?
* What do I really care about? Why?
* Who's really important to me? Why?
* Are there things that I'd like to change in the world? Or in my neighborhood? Or in my life?
* Do I pay attention to how I feel about things, activities, and people?

There are many questions you can ask yourself in addition to the ones here. Consider more specific things, like your relationships with your friends and family, for example, or what you want to be when you grow up. The questions are endless!

It's up to you whether you only want to *think* about the questions and your answers, or write about them in your diary or journal. Sometimes writing things down is helpful because you think about them more carefully and make discoveries you perhaps weren't expecting. Questions like the previous ones may lead you to express your answers through art, drama, or music. Whatever works for you is fine.

But don't answer the questions only once and then forget about them. Instead, ask the same questions at different times in your life—a month from now, six months from now, or at the beginning of the next school year. You may be surprised at what answers change and what answers don't.

It's probably clear to you that being Self Smart means you do a lot of thinking. And that means you'll have a richer and more interesting *inner life*. What's an inner life? The easiest way to answer that is to take a quick trip there.

Take about 20 minutes off from reading this book and sit in a chair, resting calmly and breathing naturally. Notice what sort of things you're aware of inside of yourself as you sit there. Are you aware of any feelings? Memories? Ideas? Sensations? Perceptions? Wishes? What else? When you look inside yourself, it's amazing to discover how much there actually is. It's as if your inner life is like the deepest ocean—huge and rich and brimming with life, with all sorts of things to look at and marvel over.

Your inner life can be a source for ideas, dreams, and creativity. Artists, writers, poets, musicians, and even scientists reach into their inner "worlds" for inspiration and answers all the time. Many religious and spiritual traditions place a high value on being Self Smart, and so do many areas of study like philosophy and psychology.

You're probably paying more visits to that ocean of inner life than you realize. How often? Try every night. Every time you dream—whether you remember it or not—you're exploring that inner life.

Do you remember your dreams? Just about everybody dreams at night, but not everybody remembers their dreams. If you'd like to remember your dreams, you can start keeping a dream journal. Keep a notebook and pencil next to your bed, and right when you wake up, write down any dreams that are still floating in your head. (You could also keep a small tape recorder by your bed and tell your dreams to it.) You might only remember bits and pieces from different dreams, or

Did You Know?

You spend roughly two hours every night in REM sleep, which is the only type of sleep you're able to dream in. During your life, you'll spend four to six years just dreaming!

you might remember entire dreams from beginning to end. The more awake you are, the greater the chance your dreams will fade. By the time you have breakfast, you've probably forgotten them (unless they were really exciting or scary). If you still don't remember your dreams, set your clock a half-hour earlier than the time you usually get up. That way, you might find yourself waking up in the middle of a dream.

Did You Know?

Many writers, scientists, mathematicians, and athletes say they've had great ideas or breakthroughs in their dreams! Robert Louis Stevenson got the idea for his book *Dr. Jekyll and Mr. Hyde* from his nightmares. (Yes, nightmares have their uses.) Famous golfer Jack Nicklaus was able to improve his golf score by practicing holding his club the way he'd held it in a dream.

Spending regular time by yourself can really help you explore the richness of what's inside of you. So it's important to give yourself time alone to do that. You can spend your alone time daydreaming, thinking, writing, drawing, walking, working on hobbies, or any of a thousand other activities that help you be more Self Smart.

Many Self Smart people are independent. They like to do things their own way and are comfortable just being themselves. Does this describe you? Being independent is a good thing—it means you value your own thoughts and ideas. But sometimes, this kind of independent thinking can take other people by surprise. Maybe they don't understand you or your goals right away. There's nothing wrong with your dreams and goals being different from those of other people's. If you have a special dream or idea—perhaps to swim with a dolphin, write a book, start your own company, travel around the world, or be a rock or rap star—pay attention and see where it takes you. Be confident that your Self Smart skills will take you places in life.

UNDERSTANDING YOUR FEELINGS

What are you feeling right now? Curious? Distracted? Excited? Worried? You might be feeling any of these or many others. An important way to be Self Smart is to recognize and understand your feelings. This can help you feel better and understand more about almost everything in your life—from how you do in school and what you want to do in the future to how you get along with friends and family. Understanding your feelings means you can make the most of your positives (being happy, succeeding at your goals) and make the negatives easier to deal with (arguing with friends, not making the school play).

Which of the following emotions have you felt in the past day?

Confident Shy Shocked

Lonesome Anxious Bored Surprised

Jealous Ashamed Cautious Happy Rowdy

Angry Mischievous Scared Peaceful

Aggressive Proud Frustrated Embarrassed

Brave Depressed Guilty Suspicious Greedy

Excited Involved Caring Loving

Curious Intrigued Safe

There are a lot of emotions to chose from, and you might be surprised at how many of them are familiar to you. Think about where and when you've felt some of these emotions recently. Are there emotions that aren't on this list that you feel often? If so, what are they?

Why is it important to think about your feelings? Because understanding them can help you *express* them. And expressing them can help you *handle* them. For example, if you're feeling enthusiastic, then you can find ways to get other people excited, too. If you're feeling lonely, you can call a friend. If you're feeling down, you can consider what might make you feel better: talking to somebody, writing in your journal, spending time outside, or whatever else comes to mind.

When you understand your feelings, you have a better chance of understanding how other people are feeling. If you've ever asked yourself,

"How would I feel if that happened to me?" then you're using your Self Smart to show *empathy*. (You may remember from Chapter 6, People Smart, empathy helps you get along better with others.)

A lot of people go around feeling angry, frustrated, scared, or upset, and *they don't even know it!* They keep feeling bad without knowing why or being able to do much about it. When you're good at knowing what you're feeling inside, it's much easier to recognize painful feelings (as well as good ones). That makes it easier to work through these emotions without taking them out on other people or letting your feelings get in the way of your dreams and goals.

Self Smart people know how to use their emotional "tools," or the things that help them handle difficult situations and feel better. Just like tools in a tool box, these tools can help you do many things. You may use all of them or only a few. And different ones might work at different times in your life. Here are some of the tools that you can use to help you understand and deal with your emotions, whatever they may be:

* **Start keeping a journal.** Your journal is a place where you can say, feel, and think anything you want—you can vent when you're angry, write down your fears, think of solutions to problems, work through being hurt or sad, or write about the things you love. You can do more than write in your journal. You can draw, write poetry, record your favorite quotes, or put designs for inventions in it. And you never have to show your journal to anyone. (Lock it up or hide it, if you need to feel extra safe about no one else reading it.)

* **Exercise.** Dancing to your favorite music, going for a long walk, running really fast, or biking in your favorite park can help you feel better. If you're mad, exercise puts all of that energy to good use and helps you blow off some steam.

* **Find someone you can talk to.** This can be a parent, best friend, neighbor, relative, friend of the family, teacher in school, or Scout

or club leader. Friends can be great to talk with about things that have you worried or upset. (If possible, have more than one person to talk to.)

* **Do something creative.** Art, music, and acting are all good ways to express yourself and work through strong emotions.

* **Be nice to yourself.** When you make a mistake or get upset about something, it's easy to be hard on yourself. Avoid saying things like: "I'm so stupid!" "Everyone hates me." "I can't do anything right." You don't want other people saying those things to you, do you? So don't say them to yourself. Instead, tell yourself positive things like: "I can learn from this mistake," or "I feel upset right now, but I can help myself feel better."

* **Go to a quiet place when you need to calm down or think about things.** This place could be a tree house, a favorite park bench, or your bedroom closet.

* **Know when you need adult help and know where to get it.** Sometimes you may have problems that are too big or scary for you to deal with on your own. For instance, if someone is hurting you (or you feel like hurting yourself or someone else), it's important to talk with a trusted adult. Some people you can talk to are parents, teachers, school counselors, clergy members, club leaders, and therapists, or call a hotline. (See page 155 for a hotline number.) If the first adult you talk to is unable to help you, keep trying. A lot of people are willing to listen and help.

* **Learn relaxation exercises or how to meditate.** If you want to learn how to meditate, a simple way to start is to sit up straight in a place where you feel comfortable and focus on your breathing for several minutes each day. (Start with five minutes, then work your way up to 10, 15, and eventually 20 minutes a day. Setting an alarm or a timer can help you time your meditation.) Pay attention to your breathing instead of anything else going on around you. As you notice your breath going in and out, you might say the word "in" as you breathe in, and "out" as you breathe out. (Or you can also count with each breath, repeating a cycle of counting from one to ten throughout your meditation time.) It's okay to notice

distracting ideas or feelings that come up, but keep returning your focus to your breathing.

* **Use what comforts you when you need it.** Maybe you have a favorite book you like to read when you're sad or a radio station or CD that you listen to when you want to relax or cheer up. You might get your comfort from a favorite stuffed toy, a hug from your mom, or even hot chocolate with marshmallows.

Did You Know?

Some people are famous for keeping journals and having them published. Anne Frank was a Jewish girl who went into hiding with her family and several others during World War II. Over the two years she was in hiding, she kept a journal detailing her thoughts, fears, and hopes for the future. Although Anne didn't survive, her journal did and is read by millions of people today. Anne Frank was a great example of a Self Smart journaler!

REACHING FOR YOUR GOALS

Being Self Smart is your greatest key to success. While you've been reading this book, you've probably made some interesting discoveries about yourself and thought, "Yep, I'm really good at that" or "I bet I can improve in this area." These self-discoveries can help you learn "smarter" for the rest your life. And building on your strengths and improving your weaknesses is what Self Smart is all about. When you work on this intelligence, you build a better *you.*

Want to know one of the best ways to improve your life right now and make your future brighter? *Setting goals.* (Of course you have to achieve them, too!) Goals can be big or small, they can be for right now or for your future. Goals can be anything you need them to be as long as they help you accomplish what you want to do. You can create goals that help you improve in math or at playing piano. Or you can create goals that will help you in the future, whether you want to study chimpanzees like Jane Goodall does in Africa or run for Congress.

Take a moment to use your Self Smart skills right now. Think about where you're going in life. Do you have an idea of what you'd like to be doing next year? How about the year after that? What about five years from now—or *10* years from now? (Does that seem like a lifetime away?)

You don't have to plan your future right this minute, but you can at least start thinking about it more often. Your future is what *you* make it—and setting goals will help get you there.

Maybe goal-setting is something you do naturally. But perhaps it isn't something you think about or do very often. Here are some important things to remember when you're setting goals for yourself:

> ## Did You Know?
>
> When Benjamin Franklin was 20 years old, he wrote down a list of goals he hoped to achieve during his life. He kept records of how he was doing over the years, and at the end of his life he was able to look back with pride on having achieved most of his goals. You might want to start even earlier than Ben Franklin and set some goals for yourself for your lifetime.

* Start by setting smaller or more short-term goals for what you hope to achieve today, or during this week, or over the next month or year. Create short-term goals (or one goal to start with) that you feel you can meet, for example, "Next week I will do 15 math problems, meet one new person, and practice my guitar for 20 minutes a day." After you succeed in these smaller goals, you'll have more confidence to take on goals that are more challenging, and that can lead to bigger and better things!

* Set goals for things you really care about. You can set goals for getting better grades, making a team, getting a role in the school play, or helping others. You can set goals for how many miles you want to bike or how many volunteer hours you want to work in a year.

* Make sure your goals are realistic. When you set impossible goals (like trying to be a millionaire by the time you turn 10), you're probably not going to be able to achieve them. You'll feel frustrated about falling short of your goals. If your goals are too big for you to achieve *right now,* build up to them. Before you can try out for the basketball team, you have to practice shooting hoops.

* Goals should be challenging. They should push you to grow and learn, to stretch your ideas of what you can achieve. If your goals are too easy, you miss out on the chance to feel good inside when

you meet them. When you reach a goal you've had to work hard for, you get a surge in self-confidence and in your abilities. If you're already good at science, but have to work hard at Spanish, then setting a goal to get an A in science doesn't make too much sense. You'll get a lot more from setting goals to improve your Spanish.

* Be specific when you set your goals. You want to know when you've reached your goals, so the more detail you add to them the better. Break down a goal into steps and actions you need to take, include when you want to reach your goal and concrete ways to tell when you've reached your goal. For example, you want a better grade in math. You have a C- and you want to get an A. Now you have a specific goal to work toward. Next, break it down into steps: Set aside an extra 45 minutes each day to work on your math homework, start a math study group with friends, and make arrangements with a teacher for extra help when you need it. Set mini-goals and bring your grades up in stages. Give yourself a deadline of the last report card of the school year to achieve your A.

You can use your goals to help you reach your dreams. Goals may need to be realistic, but they can help you achieve your most wonderful dreams. Sometimes Self Smart people have dreams that people around them may not understand (or may make fun of). Maybe you have an idea for a new invention that recycles garbage into energy or you want to write a best-selling book. Building that invention or writing that book may seem pretty unlikely now, but they're dreams you can work toward regardless what anyone else says. A lot of Self Smart people have achieved wonderful things because they believed in themselves!

But . . . what if you don't reach every goal you set for yourself? What if you try really

Did You Know?

Famous German writer Johann Wolfgang von Goethe said, "Whatever you can do, or dream you can, begin it. Boldness has genius, power, and magic in it. Begin it now."

hard but don't get exactly what you wanted? When you fall short of a goal, don't beat up on yourself. Take the opportunity to think about your goal and why you didn't achieve it. Was it realistic (bringing your grades up from C's to B's and A's by the end of the school year) or was it pretty unlikely (bringing all of your grades up from C's to A's in one report card period)?

A very important part of Self Smart is using your self-understanding to improve your life. Once you realize you're not so good at something (and it takes a lot of courage to recognize and accept that—that's also a part of being Self Smart), then you can do something positive to improve. You can make mistakes and have failures in your life and still be very Self Smart.

What's important is not that you always get everything right or succeed, but that you *learn from your mistakes or failures.* You can learn as much from your goofs as from your successes—sometimes even more! When you're Self Smart, you take what you learn and use it to make positive changes. You can do this to improve your grades in math, how fast you can run, or how well you make friends.

> ## Did You Know?
> Michael Jordan, one of the greatest sports figures in the 20th century, has had his share of failures. And this is what he has to say about them: "I've missed more than nine thousand shots in my career. Twenty-six times I've been trusted to take the game winning shot and missed. I've failed over and over and over again in my life. And that is why I succeed."

Setting goals means you're being Self Smart—you're thinking about your future, trying to improve yourself, and making your dreams come true.

Fun Ways to Become More Self Smart

Here are some ways you can expand and enjoy your Self Smart skills. Try *any* activity that appeals to you no matter how Self Smart you think you are.

1 **Ask yourself, "Who am I?"** At the top of a sheet of paper, write the words "Who Am I?" Write down as many answers to this question as you can. List your likes and dislikes, your hobbies, and anything else that comes to mind. Make your answers as detailed as possible. Take as much time and as many sheets of paper as you need.

2 **Keep a journal.** Write down your feelings, ideas, memories, or anything else you're thinking about. You can write about your day at school, an argument with a friend, or how happy you feel taking care of your cat. Write poetry or draw in your journal, if you'd like. And remember, this is *your* journal and you don't have to show it to anyone else!

3 **Make self lists.** Make a list of all the things you do well. Then make a list of all the things that you'd like to do better. Based on these lists, draw up another list of goals for yourself. (For more on goal-setting, see the next tip.)

4 **Set goals for yourself.** Pick a regular time each day, week, or month to set up specific goals that you'd like to reach over a given period of time. Set goals you can reach with some effort. If your goals are too easy, you won't feel very accomplished when you reach them. If they're too hard or impossible, you'll feel frustrated and angry because you aren't making any progress. Evaluate how you've done in meeting the goals at the end of that period, then set up new goals.

5 **Put together your autobiography.** Write or create the story of your life so far. You can use drawings, pictures, and music, or write and perform a skit or create a comic book.

6 **Create a self-collage.** Use pictures from magazines, photos, or art materials like paint markers or glitter to create a collage that expresses who you are. You can attach objects to your collage like beads, feathers, or toy cars and make the collage 3-D. Your collage can include pictures of people, things, or activities you like, or it can have pictures and objects of what you want to do in the future or of causes that are important to you. The possibilities are as endless as you are!

7 **Remember your dreams.** Find a way to keep track of your dreams at night. Write them down if you wish. Then spend time thinking about what they mean to you.

8 **Think about your day.** At the end of each day, reflect on the great things that happened, on what didn't go so well, on what you learned, and on how you can improve things in the future. Write down three things that you're thankful for or that made you happy during your day.

9 **Learn to meditate.** Take regular time to meditate by yourself. You might decide to combine your meditation with yoga. (See pages 141–142 for more about meditating.)

10 **Take a look in your Self Smart "tool box."** Make a list of all the "tools" you have to help you deal with problems and stressors in your life. These tools might include: writing in your journal, talking with a parent or close friend, meditation or relaxation exercises, deep breathing, a quiet place where you can go, or things you can do when you're sad that make you happy. (See pages 140–142 for more about what can go in your Self Smart tool box.)

11 **Read self-help books.** A lot of books can help you learn about yourself. (Some of these are listed in the resources at the end of this chapter.) You might also read books about Self Smart people who did important things because of the strength of their personal beliefs. These books could include writings by and biographies of people like Rosa Parks, Mahatma Gandhi, Martin Luther King, Eleanor Roosevelt, or Gloria Steinem.

12 **Do something you love.** Spend time each day or week by yourself doing something you love. It can be doing a hobby, volunteering for a cause you care about, or teaching yourself new things you're curious about.

13 **Start something important to you.** You might invent something (and get a patent for it) that fixes a common problem (milk jugs that are too hard to pour, for example), or you might start a business based on one of your ideas or inventions. Or you might find an issue you care a lot about—stray animals, homelessness, teaching people to read—and work for change locally or globally by doing volunteer work, starting petitions, or building a Web site with information for kids your age.

What If You Have Self-Doubts About Your Self Smarts?

Maybe you're not feeling too Self Smart right now. That's okay. Everyone—yes, everyone—has a certain amount of Self Smart ability whether they realize it or not. It's a matter of recognizing your Self Smart skills and learning to use them. Getting to know yourself can have a lot of benefits—from reaching important goals in school and life to getting along better with other people. Everything that you're already strong in can help you learn more about who you are, how you feel, and what's important to you.

And you can always use the smarts you're strongest or most comfortable in to become more Self Smart.

Here are seven ways to do it:

 If you're Word Smart: Think about what you like to read (fiction? nonfiction? mysteries? fantasy? animal books?) and reflect on what your choices say about you. Do you enjoy flights of fancy or are you more interested in the world around you? Do you read to escape or to explore other places? Think about how you connect to the characters you read about. Are your favorite characters ones that remind you of yourself or how you'd like to be? Writing is a great way to explore the answers to these questions and more. Keep a journal about the things that are important to you—your hopes for the future, how you feel, goals you have.

 If you're Music Smart: Use music to reflect, relax, and give you thinking time by listening to it or playing it. Many musicians find their music helps them understand how they're feeling or what they're thinking about. Learn an instrument that you can enjoy playing by yourself (not just with others), and remember that learning an instrument takes time—set practice goals for yourself, be patient, and stick with it!

If you're Logic Smart: Explore the world of logic on your own by working on individual logic and puzzle books. Playing with logic puzzle-toys by yourself is another good way to do this (for example, peg-board games). Choose things to learn about that are really important to you or that you feel strongly about. For example, if you care about nature or animals, study the environment and learn more about how the different parts of it work together. You'll also find that your Logic Smart skills can help you break down your goals into logical and methodical steps.

 If you're Picture Smart: Find time by yourself to create your works of art. While you're creating, reflect on your goals, your thoughts, and your ideas. All of these things can have an impact on your art and how you express yourself. What feelings would you like to express in your art? Art journals are a good way to explore and reflect on your emotions, thoughts, and fears, while being creative. When you think about your future, do you think about where you'd like to live? If you do, design and build a model of where you'd like to live when you're older.

 If you're Body Smart: Try out different solo sports (biking or swimming, for example), instead of—or in addition to—a team sport. When you find a solo sport that you enjoy, use the time when you're practicing alone to think about your day, problems, or goals, or how you feel about important things in your life. Setting goals for yourself in your sport is another way to be Self Smart. Think about what you'd like to achieve—running a faster mile or getting a new belt in martial arts—and what you need to do to reach your goal. Then go for it!

 If you're People Smart: It's great that you get along so well with people, but try to use that understanding of others to better understand yourself. What qualities do you admire in others? Do you find these qualities in yourself? What positive traits do you think you have? What traits would you like to develop and work on?

If you're Nature Smart: The next time you take a nature hike or walk, use that time to think about things going on in your life and how you feel about them. Try taking the time to reflect and even journal while you're outside in any environment. When you do this, notice what you hear, see, smell, and feel. Are your journal entries more detailed? Or do you find yourself getting distracted by other things? Does being outside affect what you think or write about?

What If You're a Self Smart Superstar?

If you know yourself really well that's great. Fortunately, there's a lot of you to know, so you always have more chances to become more Self Smart. You can explore new ways to express yourself and your feelings. You can use those Self Smart abilities of yours to learn more about the world and to grow in your other intelligences. Set your mind to it, and set goals for what you'd like to achieve or how you'd like to improve in each of your other intelligences. Figure out ways you can use them to understand yourself better or to express what you think and feel.

Your Self Smart skills can help you build your other intelligences. Here are some Self Smart ideas you can use to help you understand and develop the other intelligences in school and in life.

 For Word Smart, write your autobiography. Talking to members of your family can help you with your autobiography by giving you information about your family as a whole as well as your part in its history. Or you could write the story of how you'd like your future to look and what you want to do in it. Writing is a good way to learn more about yourself however you chose to express yourself, so experiment with creative writing—write stories, poetry, or plays about things that are important to you or about things going on in your life.

For Music Smart, create a musical autobiography using your favorite songs from when you were younger. (You could use a song for each year of your life.) You can learn a lot about yourself when you listen to music, if you think about why you're listening to it: Do you like the melody or tune? Do you like the way it makes you feel? It can make you feel good to make music, too, so learn to play or sing a song that you really like.

 For Logic Smart, look for patterns in the things you like. Do your favorite things have anything in common? If so, what? If not, why? It can be a lot of fun to learn about how your mind works, so explore the science of the mind. Find out what the different parts of the mind are and the different functions they perform. How do you see these functions in your own life? Think about personality and what makes you who you are. Do you think that you were born who you are? Or do you think that outside events and people helped make you who you are? Or both?

 For Picture Smart, experiment with the different arts to express how you feel or to create a self-portrait. Painting, drawing, collage, and papier-mâché are just a few of the ways you can express yourself visually. It may be helpful to you to try out several different kinds of art to see what you think. Which are your favorites? Do you express different feelings depending on what kind of art you're making? Another way to use your Picture Smart is to think about problems that you care about or would like to fix, and then come up with an invention that can help solve the problem. Design your invention by sketching it out, and if you can, build it.

 For Body Smart, do physical activities that let you express how you feel, like dance, acting, mime, or fine arts such as sculpture.

There are many physical activities that you can get involved with that let you focus your mind or even meditate while you get exercise, like running, bicycling, yoga, martial arts, or swimming. Meditation is also a good way to become more aware of your body and how your feelings affect it. (To learn more about how to meditate, see pages 141–142.)

 For People Smart, use how well you know yourself to get to know others better. Find people with common interests to do things with. Let your interest in issues that are important to you lead you to volunteer opportunities. When you volunteer, make a point of getting to know other volunteers and why they're there. Go to a playground or a store to people watch. See if the people you're watching are doing the same things you'd do in certain situations. If they don't, try to figure out why.

 For Nature Smart, go for a walk and take a good look around you. How does being in nature make you feel? (Happy? Peaceful? Nervous?) Why do you think you feel that way? These feelings can make really good jumping-off points for writing in your journal. Using "found objects" from nature like pinecones, leaves, and feathers (or if you're walking around in the city, find bottle caps or flyers) to create a piece of art is another way to express how you feel about nature, your environment, or anything else that's important to you.

Look to the Future

So what can you do with your Self Smart when you get older? A lot of very different things. Some of the careers you might look into include:

actor ▪ artist ▪ chaplain or member of the clergy ▪ comedian ▪ craftsperson/artisan ▪ detective/investigator ▪ film maker/director ▪ entrepreneur ▪ guidance counselor ▪ holistic health practitioner (massage therapist, acupuncturist, herbalist) ▪ inventor ▪ leader (business, political, social) ▪ performance artist ▪ personal lifestyle coach ▪ personal trainer ▪ philosopher ▪ poet ▪ professor ▪ psychiatrist ▪ psychologist ▪ researcher ▪ research scientist ▪ self-employed business person ▪ social worker ▪ teacher ▪ theologian ▪ therapist ▪ time management consultant ▪ venture capitalist ▪ writer ▪ and many more!

Get Smart with These Resources

 Books

All About Me: A Keepsake Journal for Kids by Linda Kranz (Flagstaff, AZ: Rising Moon Books, 1996). Filled with questions and jumping-off points, this journal will help you explore who you are and what you believe.

If You Had to Choose, What Would You Do? by Sandra McLeod Humphrey (Amherst, NY: Prometheus Books, 1995). This book tackles a wide variety of issues and situations and asks you what you would do in them and why.

It's All In Your Head: A Guide to Understanding Your Brain and Boosting Your Brain Power by Susan L. Barrett (Minneapolis: Free Spirit Publishing, 1992). How do you learn? How do you remember things? Can you make yourself more creative? Is there anything to ESP? Find the answers to all of these questions and more in this owner's manual for the brain written especially for kids.

The Kids' Book of Questions by Gregory Stock (New York: Workman, 1988). Poses entertaining and interesting questions designed to provoke thought and conversation. Expand your mind by answering questions such as "Do you think boys or girls have it easier?" and "Are you embarrassed by the same things that used to embarrass you?" and "If you could be invisible for a day, what would you do?"

Make Your Own Time Capsule by Steven Caney (New York: Workman, 1991). If you were going to make a time capsule for people to find in the future, what would you put in it? What objects would you choose to best represent you? Use this book to help you decide what to put in and how to prepare it. Comes with silver plastic capsule with screw-top lid.

Psychology for Kids: 40 Fun Tests That Help You Learn About Yourself by Jonni Kincher (Minneapolis: Free Spirit Publishing, 1995). Learn all about yourself, how you think, and how you make choices with these tests.

Stick Up for Yourself! Every Kid's Guide to Personal Power and Positive Self-Esteem by Gershen Kaufman, Lev Raphael, and Pamela Espeland (Minneapolis: Free Spirit Publishing, 1999). This book shows you how to make choices, be assertive, and feel better about yourself.

What Do You Really Want? How to Set a Goal and Go for It! A Guide for Teens by Beverly K. Bachel (Minneapolis: Free Spirit Publishing, 2001). Use this step-by-step guide to goal-setting to help you do anything from improving your grades in school to boosting your self-confidence to starting your own business.

What Would You Do? A Kid's Guide to Tricky and Sticky Situations by Linda Schwartz (Long Beach, CA: Learning Works, 1991). This book presents lots of different situations and then suggests ways of dealing with them: from being followed by a stranger to what to do if you find an injured animal.

Writing Down the Days: 365 Creative Journaling Ideas for Young People (Revised and Updated) by Lorraine M. Dahlstrom, M.A. (Minneapolis: Free Spirit Publishing, 2000). With a different and fresh writing idea for each day of the year, this book encourages personal responses and self-discovery.

Organizations

The Institute for Entrepreneurship
P.O. Box 26191
Milwaukee, WI 53226
(414) 302-9922
www.theeplace.org
This organization supports the creation of small businesses by kids. It holds an annual conference. A useful resource for young business people and entrepreneurs.

 Other

Girls and Boys Town National Hotline—Crisis Intervention Hotline
1-800-448-3000
www.girlsandboystown.org
Available 24 hours a day, this hotline offers crisis intervention and referrals for confronting abuse, drug problems, depression, and other difficulties. You can also visit online to chat with professional counselors, learn about nationwide recovery programs, and find further resources for moving past abuse.

Chapter 8

Nature Smart

Quick Quiz

Do you:

* like animals?
* have a "green thumb" (are good at growing plants)?
* care about nature and environmental causes?
* like going to parks, zoos, and aquariums?
* enjoy camping or hiking in nature?
* notice nature wherever you are?
* have a garden at home or in your neighborhood?
* adapt to different places and events well?
* enjoy taking care of pets (at home or in the classroom)?
* have a good memory for the details of places where you've been and the names of animals, plants, people, and things?
* ask a lot of questions about the people, places, and things you see in your environment or in nature so you can understand them better?
* have "street smarts" (the ability to understand and take of yourself in new or different situations or places)?

* pay attention to your environment in and around your neighborhood, school, and home?

* enjoy figuring out what things are and then placing them into categories (for example, bird watching or keeping a list of all the different cars you see)?

If you answered yes to any of these questions, then you just identified some of the ways you're Nature Smart!

What Does It Mean to Be Nature Smart?

When you think about Nature Smart, what's the first thing that comes to mind? Nature, most likely! Being Nature Smart means that you are curious about and understand the environment you live in. You notice what's around you and enjoy identifying and classifying things like plants or animals. You might be a weather buff, a rock hound, or a stargazer. You may be able to tell the difference between various trees, plants, animals, birds, bugs, clouds, stars, and mountains. When you're Nature Smart, you're very interested in your surroundings—wherever you happen to be.

Take a moment to think about what nature means to you. Does it mean spending as much time as possible outdoors? An interest in gardening, plants, animals, lakes and rivers, the oceans, astronomy, or the climate? Maybe it means collecting bugs, watching birds, or studying the rocks on the ground? Or is nature about living things, landscapes, or the skies? Nature is all of these things and much more—and so is being Nature Smart.

What can being Nature Smart do for you?

* You can use it to be more observant of your surroundings.

* It can help you realize the importance of the environment.

* It can help you learn more about and appreciate everything in nature.

Until modern times, Nature Smart was probably the most important kind of smart anyone could have. That's because humans had to hunt, gather plants for food or medicine, or harvest grains and other food items for survival. To do those things, people needed to understand their environment and how it worked. That meant they had to know how to raise and hunt different kinds of animals and how to gather or grow many types of plants.

When you think about it, that's an awful lot of things to know just to survive! To hunt and raise animals, you'd need to understand their habits and behaviors. You'd need the skills necessary to track the animals, too. To gather food to eat, you'd need to know which plants were poisonous and which ones were okay to eat. (And you definitely wouldn't want to make any mistakes!) Your knowledge of plants would also need to include which ones had the ability to heal and how to use them for medicine. If you were growing plants for food, you'd have to know when and where to plant them, how much sun and water they needed, and how to get rids of any bugs that wanted to eat your crops before you could.

All of these important abilities—observation, understanding the environment, getting along

Did You Know?

In many parts of the world today, for example, in the rainforests around the Amazon River and Papua New Guinea, there are still people who can tell the differences between tens of thousands of different kinds of plants (even those that look almost identical to an outside observer). Some of these people are real wizards with herbs and can recognize and use hundreds of different medicinal herbs and plants for curing diseases or treating accidents.

with animals, and being able to grow things—are the basis for Nature Smart. Today, many people use their Nature Smart abilities when they identify different types of plants or animals. Some people can look at a leaf, for example, and tell you what kind of tree it came from. Other people can look at an animal track on the ground and tell you what kind of animal left it. Although you may not need skills like these to survive in today's world, you've still got Nature Smart abilities—even if you live in a city.

Things you may do every day that use this intelligence:

hike ▪ learn everything you can about dinosaurs ▪ visit science or nature museums, zoos, or aquariums ▪ go for a walk in the park ▪ care for a family or class pet ▪ collect leaves, bugs, rocks, feathers, or other things found in nature ▪ bird watch ▪ take nature walks ▪ have an aquarium, terrarium, or ant farm ▪ pay attention to the weather ▪ walk a dog ▪ volunteer at the Humane Society ▪ grow a garden or house plants ▪ cook ▪ look at the stars

EXPLORING YOUR WORLD

Nature Smart is about paying attention to the natural world in all of its forms and learning to understand it. Your favorite way to learn about nature may be to get out in it and examine the wild creatures that live there. Depending on what part of the world you live in, you might spot squirrels, crows, lizards, pigeons, iguanas, wild boar, horses, cows, or deer. You might also see daisies, roses, ferns, oak trees, cacti, palm trees, canyons, hills, mountains, valleys, deserts, or any of a million other natural things.

Do you have a special place in nature where you go when you need to get away from it all? Maybe you take some binoculars so you can do a little bird or animal watching. Maybe you bring a camera to take pictures of beautiful or

Did You Know?

There are people living in hunter cultures (for example, the Gikwe bushmen of the Kalahari in Africa) who can look at animal tracks and droppings and tell you not only what kind of animal it was, but whether it was male or female, what direction it was going, how long ago since it had been there, and even what the animal had for breakfast!

interesting scenes. Maybe you prefer to sketch in a notebook or carry along a backpack or bag for collecting samples of leaves, rocks, feathers, or flowers. Maybe you like to think, dream, and reflect while you're in this special place.

If you live in an urban area or someplace in the suburbs, you might wonder, "How can I be Nature Smart if I'm not around nature all the time?" The good news is that Nature Smart is adaptable. Even if you spend all of your time in a city instead of on a farm, you can use your abilities to notice your unique surroundings. For example, someone who's Nature Smart may know all of the ins and outs of the neighborhood— what the best shortcuts are, where the bus routes go, or which stores sell the coolest comic books. Does this sound like you? If you're a city dweller, you probably don't see a lot of animal tracks but maybe you use your Nature Smarts to identify different types of sneakers, CD covers, or automobiles. (You use those old "hunter/gatherer" skills for man-made things instead.)

Even if you live in a large city, there may be more nature around you than you think—patio gardens, ants on the sidewalk, pigeon nests on the ledges of tall buildings. To explore your Nature Smart abilities further, you might:

* Join an urban garden club. You can work in a garden and maybe get your own patch to grow whatever you want.
* Go to a farmers' market to buy vegetables, fruit, or flowers.
* Visit local parks in your city. Go to nature museums, science museums, aquariums, or zoos.
* Raise houseplants or grow a patio garden. (Maybe you can take care of plants in your classroom, too.)
* Get a kit and build your own worm farm or ant farm.
* Keep low-maintenance pets like fish or hermit crabs. Or get an aquarium and create an entire underwater ecosystem with fish, plants, and snails.

* Create a terrarium. Terrariums are small indoor gardens with several different varieties of slow-growing plants. They are usually enclosed and can be created in a variety of different containers including jars and aquariums. Some people create partially open terrariums and have animals such as lizards, snakes, or frogs in them.

* Read books about animals. They can be nonfiction or stories with animals as characters.

* Collect rocks or shells. (If you can't collect them in person, you can still buy them and learn about them.)

* Learn about a recycling program in your neighborhood. If you can, find a way to volunteer for it. If there isn't any recycling where you live, think about what a program would need to do and who you could talk to about starting one. Or start a recycling program at your school.

* Learn about environmental issues and problems. You can study about the environment, write letters to leaders about it, and sign petitions (documents with people's signatures on them in support of or against an issue that are sent to people making decisions about that issue), no matter where you live.

* Plant a tree. Trees help clean up the air, provide places for animals to live, and are just nice to have around. Good places to plant trees are at your school, your neighborhood, and local parks. Many areas have tree-planting programs in the spring or fall, or on Arbor Day.

* Volunteer to be summer caretaker for a class pet, or talk to your teacher about going on field trips to a zoo, a science museum, or a wildlife area.

* Look to the sky. Watch the birds flying overhead. Study the stars and pay attention to the weather.

CARING ABOUT THE EARTH

You may show your Nature Smart in the most basic way of all—by your love of the outdoors. You may love going on hikes, camping trips, canoeing, or doing any activity that you can do outside. Some people find ways to spend their lives outdoors. They may find jobs that let them be outdoors—park rangers who protect nature for future generations, field biologists who study animals in their habitats, or landscape designers who create beautiful gardens for people.

People who love the outdoors may spend their lives exploring, learning about, and educating others about places that most people will never see like Antarctica or the Amazon rainforests. And there are people who spend their time traveling and having adventures in nature—sailing around the world, bicycling down the coast of South America, kayaking around the Great Lakes, or climbing the Himalayas.

Clearly, not everyone goes on adventures in nature. It's actually pretty easy to fall out of touch with the natural world in your daily life. More people every year are living in cities and suburbs. As cities and suburbs grow, large pieces of land that use to be farms or wilderness (nesting areas, grazing pastures, and feeding grounds) have been replaced with housing developments, malls, and factories. With fewer people living on farms and ranches, most people aren't growing, raising, or killing their own food anymore. Instead, they buy their food at the grocery store. Under these circumstances, it's not too surprising that many people have lost touch with the natural world in their daily lives.

But this has given rise to a new subtype of Nature Smart—something I call "eco-smart." This is the desire to take care of the natural places and living things that are disappearing in the modern world. People who are eco-smart are finding ways to protect the environment and preserve it for future generations.

Maybe eco-smart is where your Nature Smart gifts truly bloom. Maybe you've been involved in a recycling campaign, a litter removal project, or efforts to protect animals or endangered species in your region. You might be working to get toxic waste cleaned up in your town or are involved in efforts to save the oceans and rainforests around the world. If any of this sounds like you, then you could even think of yourself as an "earth angel," or someone who loves the planet and wants to save it from destruction.

You can take care of your environment wherever you live. Here are some ways to do it:

* **Recycle.** Tons and tons of trash are created each year. You and your family can help by buying products with less packaging and by recycling as many things as possible. Paper, cans, and bottles are usually the easiest to recycle. Plastics of all kinds can be recycled, too. You might be surprised at some of the other things you can recycle and how you can do it. Clothes, books, furniture, and many other things can be recycled by giving them to people who need them. You can donate these things to organizations that run thrift shops to raise money, or to places like homeless or women's shelters. If you've ever worn hand-me-downs from your older brothers or sisters, you were recycling.

* **Repair and reuse things.** Think twice before you throw something away. Can it be fixed? Is there a way for you to reuse it or give it to someone who can?

* **Act locally.** There are plenty of environmental issues in your own neighborhood and region you can get involved with and learn about. From saving wetlands to starting a recycling program at your school, there are a variety of things you can do to help.

* **Act globally.** Actions that harm the environment anywhere in the world have an impact on every other place in the world. What that means is that it doesn't have to happen in *your* neighborhood for it to be a problem for your neighborhood. Stay aware of what's going on around the world by watching the news and reading about the

issues. Many environmental organizations have a global focus and are good places to learn about important issues, sign petitions, and find out who you can write to about your concerns.

CARING FOR PLANTS

Perhaps you have a "green thumb," or a real gift for growing plants. You show your Nature Smart by caring for living, growing things. Maybe you grow flowers in a window box or tomatoes in a container on your patio. You may have a little piece of land where you raise and tend a vegetable garden in your yard or in a community garden. Or perhaps you're the one in your family or school who's responsible for watering and feeding the plants around the home or classroom, because everyone knows you're the one who will take the best care of the plants (and maybe even talk to them to help them grow).

Growing plants takes Nature Smart know-how—like knowing how much sun, water, or fertilizer each plant may need. On top of knowing about the care and feeding of plants, some Nature Smart people have a little something extra, a "green feeling" for living things that helps them provide a special nurturing touch to everything they grow.

Did You Know?

Someone once called the naturalist Luther Burbank, "the man who talked to plants" because he was so good at making them grow!

Even if you don't have a green thumb, you can still love plants and learn how to grow them successfully. If you live in a city, window boxes are a great way to grow flowers and herbs. You can cook with the herbs you grow. If you can find space for a garden, you can experiment with growing all kinds of things. Larger flowers such as sunflowers and vegetables such as tomatoes, peppers, and lettuce are all easy plants to start with.

If you discover that you enjoy growing the basics, you can expand your garden to include just about anything you're curious about: green beans or snap peas that climb up poles, strawberries that thrive in terrace pots, or pumpkins for your own jack-o-lanterns. And with every new plant you put in your garden, the more you learn and the more Nature Smart you become.

After you grow all those fruits and vegetables, what are you going to do with them? Eat them, of course! There's nothing quite as tasty as homegrown tomatoes or fresh-picked raspberries from your own patch, so if you like growing food for your family and friends, you may also enjoy learning to prepare meals. Lots of Nature Smart people turn out to be great cooks. Imagine seasoning a sauce with herbs you grew yourself or putting together salads with your own fruits and vegetables. It's fun to experiment—and you and all your friends and family will appreciate the "fruits of your labor."

CARING FOR ANIMALS

If you love animals, you're Nature Smart. You may never have thought about it that way, but it's true. (You might even be the kid in your neighborhood who always ends up finding hurt or lost animals and figuring out ways to help them.) Maybe you never realized that caring for animals is a form of intelligence.

There are many different ways that animals can be part of your life. If you live on a farm or a ranch, you and your family may work with animals, breed them, and even raise them for food.

You may care about animals and demonstrate it by volunteering at the Humane Society walking dogs or playing with cats. You might show your concern for animals by being a *vegetarian* (someone who doesn't eat meat or fish). Or you might take care of animals by tending to the family pets, adopting strays, or helping any hurt animals you come across. Whether you look after them, raise them, or simply learn as much as you can about them, you're showing your Nature Smart skills.

If you love animals, you may have a pet—or even several of them. You might have cats and dogs, hamsters or gerbils, fish in an aquarium, or a horse or pony in a stable. You may have more exotic pets like lizards, snakes, or tarantulas. Owning and taking care of pets is one of the most common ways that people show their love of animals. When you take care of pets, you're taking responsibility for their well-being. You're making sure that they are fed, watered, and walked. You keep their litter boxes or cages cleaned; you keep them happy by playing with them, cuddling or petting them, and just spending time with them. If you can't have a pet of your own, you may really enjoy playing with friends' pets or taking care of classroom pets at school.

Some people relate to animals better than to human beings. You may know somebody like that, or maybe you're like that yourself. You may understand why the animals around you do what they do and even learn to communicate with them. Monty Roberts, a man who is known as the real-life "Horse Whisperer," has been riding and working with horses since he was a small child. When he was 7 years old, he realized that horses communicated with each other in very specific ways. He started trying to communicate with horses in the same ways they communicated with each other—using similar body movements and actions. His efforts worked and he developed a reputation for being able to gently tame wild or unhappy horses that no one else had any luck with.

> ## Did You Know?
>
> There's a woman in Colorado named Dr. Temple Grandin who has difficulty relating to humans (she has something called "autism" that causes problems with her interactions with other people), but she understands livestock really well. She's become world famous for understanding how animals like cattle, sheep, and pigs think and for designing ways to handle and move them without upsetting them. She even tests the final designs on herself!

Many people who work closely with animals, including veterinarians, animal trainers, and scientists, seem to have an uncanny ability to communicate with them. Jane Goodall is a scientist who has studied chimpanzees in Africa for most of her life. She lived around the tribes of chimpanzees she's studied for generations, learned their body language, and witnessed chimp activities that no one else had ever seen before. She has spent so much time around them that she is able to think like them! Now, she is going around the world visiting schools and talking to kids in many countries about the importance of preserving the habitats of chimpanzees and other animals from destruction by poachers (people who hunt illegally or hunt endangered species), farmers, and developers (people who purchase land—including habitats—to build on it).

Working with and caring for animals isn't limited to the animals that live on land. Trainers work closely with orcas (killer whales), dolphins, and sea lions to create complicated and entertaining programs at water parks. All of these animals are noted for their intelligence, curiosity, and their ability to communicate.

Dolphins and whales are especially known for how they communicate among themselves. There are scientists who study *bioacoustics,* or the sounds that other species use to communicate. These scientists and marine biologists have observed many kinds of whales and dolphins to learn how they communicate with each other in their pods, or social and family groups. Some scientists are even trying to figure out if orcas and humans can learn to communicate with each other. There are many ways that Nature Smart people can turn their love of living things into really cool careers—someday you might, too!

Did You Know?

Dogs can help you read better. The libraries in Salt Lake City, Utah, have started a program called R.E.A.D.® (Reading Education Assistance Dogs). Kids ages 5 to 9 come in and read aloud to dogs of all different breeds and sizes (and the dogs' handlers) for 30 minutes every Saturday. Reading test scores for kids who read to a Pet Partner® team (a dog and handler) went up two levels or more!

Whether you live in the city or the country, you probably have had some memorable experiences with nature: having a class pet, catching insects, digging in the dirt or building sandcastles on the beach, bringing home a flower that you picked, planting seeds to watch them grow. There are probably as many different ways to be Nature Smart as there are things in nature.

As you begin to explore this intelligence further, you might take a new interest in the stars or the weather. Or you might be drawn to the ground beneath your feet and develop a real passion for rocks, minerals, or fossils. You might be curious about lakes and oceans and all the things that live and grow in them. The whole world is yours to explore and learn about when you're being Nature Smart.

Fun Ways to Become More Nature Smart

Here are some ways that you can expand and enjoy your Nature Smart skills. Try *any* activity that appeals to you no matter how Nature Smart you think you are.

1 **Notice nature wherever you are.** Maybe it's watching ants being industrious on the playground blacktop, noting the different flowers and vegetables growing in the community garden, enjoying the changing leaves on the trees in a local park in the fall, or studying the surprisingly complex ecosystem you know as your backyard.

2 **Plant something and watch it grow.** You could plant a flower, a pepper plant, or any plant that interests you. Notice the different stages your plant goes through as it grows. How quickly does it grow? How much water does it need? Does it like lots of sun? Do these things change as it gets bigger?

3 **Lie down in your yard and look at the sky.** On a sunny afternoon, notice the different kinds of clouds in the sky. Are they thin and streaky? Fluffy? Are they still? Or is the wind blowing them across the sky? What can you tell about the weather? Does it look like there might be rain coming in?

4 **Look at the sky on a clear night.** What color is the sky? You may be able to see stars and even planets. Often Venus and Mars are can be seen on or near the horizon. Look at the moon and see if you can tell what stage it's at. Is it a full moon? Is it waxing (moving from a crescent moon to becoming a full moon)? Or is it waning (shrinking from a full moon to a crescent moon)? You may also be able to see shooting stars (this is easier with darker skies). If you're in the city, it may be too light to see many stars. If so, what else can you see? Planes? Helicopters? Building lights?

5 **If you like looking at the stars, learn the constellations.** Constellation are groups of stars that look like objects (The Big Dipper), animals (Taurus), or people (Gemini, the Twins). Most constellations have stories to explain them. These stories from different cultures often tell how the constellations (or the people or animals they represent) got up into the sky. Try identifying the constellations at night or make your own on your bedroom ceiling with glow-in-the-dark stars. You could even make a simple planetarium for yourself by poking the shapes of constellations into a black piece of construction paper, and then shining a flashlight up through the paper onto the ceiling of a dark room. Maybe you want to look for your own constellations in the sky and write stories about them.

6 **Start a garden.** If you don't have a yard, try growing a window-box garden of flowers or herbs. Help to plan, dig, plant, nurture, and harvest a garden at home or as part of your school. If your neighborhood has a community garden, get a little patch of your own.

7 **Start a community garden.** Get together with other kids, teens, and grown-ups in your neighborhood and start a community garden. This might involve cleaning and fixing up a vacant lot before you can plant anything. A community garden can have flowers, vegetables, fruit, or herbs—anything that a garden member wants to plant.

8 **Go bird watching.** Get some binoculars and go out to a wooded area near your home or school and observe the different types of birds in your region. Bring along a guidebook so you can identify any unfamiliar birds you may see.

9 **Watch nature shows on television.** *Nature, Nova,* and *National Geographic* on PBS are good places to start. If you have access to cable, then the Discovery Channel, the Learning Channel, and Animal Planet are all good places to find shows about nature. If you can, watch these shows with your family or friends and discuss what you see.

10 **Read books and magazines about nature.** Look for books about animals, dinosaurs, or rainforests (or any part of nature that you're curious about). You might be interested in reading about the lives of famous naturalists such as: John Muir, Rachel Carson, Charles Darwin, George Washington Carver, and Jane Goodall. Good magazines to check out are *National Geographic for Kids, Ranger Rick,* and *Contact 3-2-1.*

11 **Get involved with an environmental organization.** You can work with a local group that focuses on issues important to where you live or get involved with a group that tackles national or even international issues. Groups like Greenpeace, the Sierra Club, Earth Island Institute, and the World Wildlife Fund all work on a variety of environmental issue from pollution and reducing pesticide use to protecting endangered species and habitats.

12 **Volunteer for a "green" school or community project.** You could work for a community recycling program, raise awareness about saving the rain forests or coral reefs, plant trees, communicate with classrooms around the world about their local environmental issues, or study endangered species.

13 **Take care of a pet.** Be the person in charge of raising and taking care of a family or classroom pet. This means you feed it, give it water, walk it, clean out its litter box or cage, and wash it. Is taking care of a pet more work and responsibility than you first thought? Do you know more about your pet after taking care of it for a while?

14 **Build your own ecosystem.** Put together an aquarium, terrarium, ant farm, or some other portable ecosystem. There's a lot to learn about what goes into an ecosystem, no matter how small it is. Every plant, animal, and bug plays a role. If you can't have one at home, talk with your teacher about building one as a class science project.

15 **Learn about an animal.** Select a particular species that you're curious about—you can choose a domestic animal like a dog, cat, or pig, or a more exotic animal like a snow leopard, wombat, or oryx. Learn as much about the animal as you can. If it's a domestic animal, you could learn about the different breeds and their origins and how it got domesticated in the first place. If it's an exotic animal, learn about its habitat, whether it's endangered and why, and what role it plays in the ecosystem.

16 **Visit a natural history museum, zoo, aquarium, or arboretum.** From planetariums to botanical gardens, there are many places where you can learn more about nature. Many museums run special educational programs about local plants and animals, sky-watching, or other topics.

17 **Look at the ground beneath your feet.** You can learn a lot about where you live from dirt and rocks. You can find different kinds of minerals and even fossils in some regions. Read about the geology of your local area, and then look for examples of the rocks, minerals, and other things you may have read about. If you get really interested, start a rock collection and use rock and mineral handbooks or guides to help you identify what you've collected.

18 **Get out in nature.** If you can, go to a camp, take a backpacking trip, or go on a day hike. Make opportunities to learn something new about the natural world around you. Keep a naturalist's journal of the different things you are learning about, and sketch or take pictures of plants, animals, or natural formations to go along with your journal entries.

19 **Start a collection.** Bugs of all kinds, leaves, flowers, and rocks can all be good things to collect. You can press the leaves and flowers between the pages of books and place them in scrapbooks. If the idea of killing the bugs you collect doesn't appeal to you, make a temporary bug collection, where you catch the bugs in a jar with air holes in it and then release your collection at the end of the day or evening. No matter what your interest, there are books and clubs where you can learn more about it. But remember to be careful when you're collecting not to hurt the environment by collecting things that are better left in place.

20 **Learn how to cook.** There are lots of fun things you can learn to make, and cooking can be more fun if you're using herbs and vegetables that you've grown yourself.

What If You're Not "Wild" About Your Nature Smart Skills?

Maybe animals make you nervous, camping makes you queasy, and plants practically wilt when you walk by. It's probably not that bad, but you may not feel really Nature Smart either. You can polish up your Nature Smart abilities everywhere you go (and no matter where you live).

The most important thing you can do to become more Nature Smart is to be more observant. *Notice* everything that's around you. Look at the sky and see the stars, the clouds, or how the angle of the sun changes with the seasons. Look at the ground and notice the rocks, the color of the dirt, and the different kinds of bugs. And of course there are all kinds of animals, birds, trees, and flowers to observe in between. Nature's everywhere you turn, and there are so many different things in it that make up your environment.

Being more observant will not only help you become more Nature Smart, it can give you writing ideas if you're Word Smart, art inspirations if you're Picture Smart, and science experiment ideas if you're Logic Smart. And that's just scratching the surface. So it pays to pay attention, no matter what intelligences you feel best about.

And you can always use the smarts you're strongest or most comfortable in to become more Nature Smart.

Here are seven ways to do it:

 If you're Word Smart: Get closer to nature by reading about it or by reading stories with animals as characters. When you're reading in general, notice how environments and natural settings contribute to the story. If you want to write, use nature or environmental issues as a theme for a story, poem, or play. A great way to get started is to take a notebook with you the next time you go for a walk and write about the things you see around you.

 If you're Music Smart: Listen for music in natural sounds like wind blowing, birds singing, or even cars whooshing by. There can literally be a whole world of inspiration for you in the sounds around you for songs and melodies. You could turn your hand to writing songs about the environment. (There's a long tradition of songwriters writing about issues that are important to them—join it!)

If you're Logic Smart: Look for patterns, numbers, and logic in nature. For instance, you could practice estimating how many of something (fire hydrants? dogs? dandelions?) you'll see before you go on a walk. Searching for geometric shapes in natural settings can be another way to find patterns. Nature also provides a lot of opportunities to solve problems in real-world settings. For example, you could estimate how many peppers are in your garden if you need some for a pizza you're making or figure out how tall a tree is if it's in danger of falling on nearby playground equipment.

If you're Picture Smart: Use natural materials in your art. Leaves, flowers, seed pods, and feathers are just a few of the things you might be able to use in your art. You could incorporate them into your art or use them to make your art. Try painting with feathers or making "nature stamps" out of leaves and rocks, or even vegetables and fruit! Nature can be a source of art ideas as well, so experiment with painting, sketching, or drawing pictures based on items you see in natural settings. For instance, take a good look—a really good look—at a single flower, insect, or crack in the sidewalk and recreate it in your own artistic way.

If you're Body Smart: Go walking, jogging, in-line skating, or biking through your neighborhood, a state park, or another area by yourself or with friends or family. (Make sure you know what equipment is allowed on any given trail.) It can be a lot of fun to visit new places or nature areas. Sharing your impressions and finding out what other people are seeing could help you notice more things, so talk about what you're seeing in the environment while you're enjoying the fresh air!

If you're People Smart: You can combine your love of people with nature by enjoying the outdoors with others (whether it's in a forest, by an ocean, in the city, or in the country). You can have fun and even socialize in nature by going on a picnic with your family in a neighborhood or state park. Hiking and going for walks with your friends can be a great way to get out in nature. If you'd like to learn more about the area where you live, talk with neighbors, store clerks, and others to learn about your neighborhood and region.

 If you're Self Smart: Nature can be a great place to think about what's important to you, so take a reflective walk in the woods, in the country, or in your neighborhood. You can learn a lot about yourself and the world around you. Take in everything using all of your senses—what do you see, hear, smell, or feel? Bring a journal or sketch book along to write down your thoughts about nature and what you see.

What If You're a Nature Smart Natural?

Maybe you've been a vegetarian since the age of 6, take care of the family cats, and recycle anything you can get your hands on. What else can you do? You can always learn more about environmental causes around the world and take advantage of volunteer opportunities where you live. Get other people involved and aware. For example, organize a school clean-up day to pick up litter, clean up graffiti, and plant trees and flowers. Talk with your school about setting up a school vegetable garden. The garden could be a class science project and the vegetables could be donated to local food banks or homeless shelters.

Your Nature Smart skills can help you build your other intelligences. Here are some Nature Smart ideas you can use to help you understand and develop the other intelligences in school and in life.

For Word Smart, raise awareness about environmental causes that are important to you by making presentations in classes, writing letters to the editor, or making up raps. You can use your Word Smart skills to explore nature in general, too, by writing and reading stories that feature nature or have animals in them. Many poets have found inspiration in nature, so maybe you can, too. Write poetry about your favorite things in nature. If you already keep a journal, start noting your thoughts and ideas about everything you observe that interests you in nature.

For Music Smart, you may already hear music in nature, so try listening for nature in music. Does the percussion in a song remind you of rain on a roof? Does a flute sound like a bird call? Or a piano solo like water going over rocks? Many instruments and songs were inspired by sounds in nature. See if you can figure out what the original inspirations were. Let nature inspire you to make music with improvised instruments—for example, sticks, stones in a container, water in glasses.

For Logic Smart, ask questions about and look for answers in nature. Those same observation skills that make you so great at solving math or logic problems and coming up with science experiments are just as great for exploring nature. In fact, many types of scientists rely on both Logic Smart and Nature Smart, so do a special project in your science class at school that relates in some way to the life sciences: biology, botany, zoology, entomology (bugs), ornithology (birds). Or you can combine math and logic with nature by looking for examples of math and patterns in nature and then researching or coming up with your own theories to explain what you see.

For Picture Smart, pay attention to what you see in nature—the colors, the patterns, the textures. You might be surprised at what you notice. Do you see art in nature? Do your observations make you want to make art of your own using nature? Use things you like in nature to practice your art skills—draw your cat or your favorite flower, make a model of your favorite place in nature.

For Body Smart, use getting out in nature as an excuse to get some exercise. Hike, bike, run, skate, or walk out in nature. While you're getting all that exercise, pay attention to what's around you and notice how nature appeals to your physical senses—the sounds of birds, the smells of flowers, or the feel of dirt between your toes. There are other ways to get active with nature like digging in a garden, training a dog, or helping to clean up your favorite park where you like to play or run.

 For People Smart, you can use the things that are most important to you—animals, the environment, gardening—to reach out to others. A good way to start is by volunteering your time and energy to work with others on environmental causes. Or organize your friends and clean up your school grounds or a local park. If you love animals, find a program that brings animals into hospitals or rest homes for visits and get involved. You'll become closer with your animal companion and get to meet a lot of people who are excited to visit with you and your four-footed pal.

 For Self Smart, use nature to help you understand what you're feeling. Pay attention to what you're thinking about the next time you're taking a walk. Are you analyzing what you see? Admiring its beauty? If you find you enjoy nature, set and meet goals about things you'd like to do to help the environment (recycle more, become a vegetarian, write a letter a week in support of environmental issues) or things you can do to get into a nature-based career (study science, volunteer at the natural history museum, talk with park rangers about how they got their jobs).

Look to the Future

So what can you do with your Nature Smart when you get older? A lot of very different things. Some of the careers you might look into include:

animal trainer ▪ archeologist ▪ astronomer ▪ beekeeper ▪ biologist ▪ botanist ▪ chef/cook ▪ ecologist ▪ entomologist (someone who studies bugs) ▪ environmental/ecological advocate ▪ environmental inspector ▪ environmental lawyer ▪ environmental scientist ▪ farmer ▪ fisher ▪ forensic scientist ▪ forest/park ranger ▪ gamekeeper ▪ garden nursery owner/employee ▪ gardener ▪ geologist ▪ herpetologist (someone who studies reptiles such as lizards, snakes, and crocodiles) ▪ horticulturist ▪ ichthyologist (studies fish) ▪ landscape designer ▪ marine biologist ▪ meteorologist ▪ mountaineer ▪ naturalist ▪ natural resources manager ▪ nature guide/interpreter ▪ nature photographer ▪ ornithologist (someone who studies birds) ▪ paleontologist (someone who studies fossils) ▪ physical anthropologist ▪ rancher ▪ sailor ▪ tree surgeon ▪ veterinarian ▪ veterinary assistant ▪ vulcanologist (someone who studies vocanoes) ▪ zookeeper ▪ zoologist ▪ and many more!

Get Smart with These Resources

 Books and Magazines

Backyard Explorer Kit by Rona Beame (New York: Workman, 1989). This book focuses on tree and leaf identification, with examples of all of the major leaf and needle shapes. Kit includes a heavy plastic collecting envelope and a collecting album.

Birds Every Child Should Know by Neltje Blanchan (Iowa City: University of Iowa Press, 2000). This classic guide will help you identify more than 100 common birds.

Exploring the Night Sky: The Equinox Astronomy Guide for Beginners by Terrence Dickerson (Buffalo, NY: Firefly Books, 1988). This award-winning guide for beginning astronomers teaches you how to identify planets, stars, and constellations and how to stargaze from the city as well as the country.

Fun with Nature: Take-Along Guide by Mel Boring, Diane L. Burns, and Leslie A. Dendy (Minocqua, WI: NorthWord Press, 1999). Take this book with you on your nature walks and use it to identify more than 150 different plants and animals.

National Geographic Kids (formerly *National Geographic World*)
Explore rainforests and volcanoes, learn about endangered species, and travel to new places around the world in the pages of this magazine. Filled with fascinating photographs, articles, maps, projects, puzzles and games, and pullout posters.

Rocks and Fossils (An Usborne Guide) by Martyn Bramwell, Ian Jackson, and Alan Suttie (Newton, MA: EDC Publications, 1994). This book, complete with magnifying glass and rocks in a vinyl bag, helps you learn how to identify and gather rocks and fossils.

 Organizations

Greenpeace
P.O. Box 7939
Fredericksburg, VA 22404
1-800-326-0959
www.greenpeaceusa.org/green/clubhouse.htm
An organization dedicated to the preservation of the environment, Greenpeace concentrates on issues like global warming, pollution in the oceans, and toxic and nuclear wastes. Visit the Kids' Clubhouse site listed above to learn amazing earth facts, view art from kids, and play games that help you stay informed on environmental issues.

Kids F.A.C.E.—Kids for A Clean Environment
P.O. Box 158254
Nashville, TN 37215
(615) 331-7381
www.kidsface.org
Kids F.A.C.E. is a free club for kids and teachers to help kids learn more about nature and get involved with activities that are good for the environment. Contact them for information on starting a chapter in your area.

National Geographic Society
1145 17th Street NW
Washington, DC 20036
1-800-647-5463
www.nationalgeographic.com/kids

The world's largest nonprofit scientific and educational organization, the National Geographic Society works to inform people about the wonder of the natural world. They have a magazine for kids called *National Geographic Kids*. Check out their kids' Web site listed above to find cool facts, games, puzzles, coloring books, comics, maps, recipes, videos, discussions, and more about nature and the environment. They also have a section for homework help.

National Wildlife Federation

11100 Wildlife Center Drive
Reston, VA 20190
1-800-822-9919
www.nwf.org/kids
The National Wildlife Federation works with individuals, organizations, businesses, and the government to protect wildlife and the environment. At the kids' site, you'll find games, quizzes, articles, homework help, cyber-nature tours, links to other environmental and wildlife organizations, and more.

Roots and Shoots Program

Jane Goodall Institute
8700 Georgia Avenue, Suite 500
Silver Spring, MD 20910
(240) 645-4000
www.janegoodall.org
The Roots and Shoots Program for young people was started by Jane Goodall, a famous primatologist (someone who studies monkeys and apes) and environmentalist. Learn about the environment and what you can do to protect it locally and globally.

World Wildlife Fund

P.O. Box 97180
Washington, DC 20090-7180
1-800-225-5993
www.worldwildlife.org/fun/kids.cfm
The World Wildlife Fund is dedicated to protecting the wildlife and habitats of the world. Their Kid's Stuff Web site teaches about biodiversity and endangered species around the world and in your own backyard. It has fun factsheets, games, quizzes, pictures, and a homework helper.

 ## Web Sites

Kid's Valley Garden

www.raw-connections.com/garden
This excellent site covers all of the basics from planning and planting, to keeping your plants healthy and entering them in shows. Learn about veggies, herbs, and flowers as well as bugs and how to create a compost heap. There's a glossary and lots of great links.

Playing It Smart Every Day

Congratulations on finishing the book! I hope you've learned a lot of new things. You may feel a little overwhelmed by all the new information you've discovered. If you do, remember that you have your entire life to develop, understand, and enjoy all of your different smarts. It's great that you've started exploring and working on them now. This will help you as you continue to grow and learn in your teens and well beyond.

What you're good at and enjoy doing now may turn out to be a guide for what you study and even do for a living in the future. Maybe you're especially Word Smart and love to write, yet you're also very visual (Picture Smart) and love nature (Nature Smart). You might become a travel writer or a science fiction writer who creates new worlds for readers to explore.

You'll probably always notice that some of your intelligences are stronger or more comfortable for you. Some of them may develop more rapidly than others or at different times in your life. For example, you may not think of yourself as very Logic Smart now, but in 20 years you might find yourself in a job that really pushes you to build up your Logic Smart abilities. And you may find that not only are you stronger in Logic Smart than you thought, but you really enjoy it, too!

As you continue to develop your intelligences, researchers are finding out more about the different kinds of smart. The Theory of Multiple Intelligences suggests that it's possible there are other intelligences that haven't been identified yet. (More ways for you to be smarter than you think!) There's at least one more intelligence on the horizon right now: Existential Intelligence, which asks big questions like "What's the purpose of life?" and "What happens after we die?" People who are strong in this smart may be involved in religion or philosophy or look for answers to these questions through their art, writing, and science. You may already see signs of this intelligence in yourself, even as researchers are looking for more information about it. What other kinds of smart do you think there are?

Learning about all of your different smarts is a great adventure—one that will last a lifetime. You're off to a smart start!

Index

About the Author

Thomas Armstrong, Ph.D., is an award-winning author and speaker with 30 years of teaching experience and over one million copies of his books in print. He has authored 11 books, including *Multiple Intelligences in the Classroom;* written numerous articles for *Parenting, Ladies' Home Journal, Family Circle,* and other periodicals; and appeared on several national and international television and radio programs, from NBC's the *Today* show to the BBC. He lives in Sonoma County, California, with his wife Dr. Barbara Turner, a psychotherapist, and their two Shih Tzu dogs Aladdin and Rosie.

Fast, Friendly, and Easy to Use

www.freespirit.com

Browse the catalog

Info & extras

Many ways to search

Quick check-out

Stop in and see!

To place an order or to request a free catalog of SELF-HELP FOR KIDS® and SELF-HELP FOR TEENS® materials, please write, call, email, or visit our Web site:

Free Spirit Publishing Inc.
217 Fifth Avenue North • Suite 200 • Minneapolis, MN 55401-1299
toll-free 800.735.7323 • local 612.338.2068 • fax 612.337.5050
help4kids@freespirit.com • www.freespirit.com